Life Skills and Success Tips

A Teen Handbook

David Cowan and Dianne Schilling

Cover design: Dave Cowan
Illustrations: Dianne Schilling

ISBN-10: 1-56499-086-9

ISBN-13: 978-1-56499-086-0

INNERCHOICE Publishing
15079 Oak Chase Court
Wellington, FL 33414

www.InnerchoicePublishing.com

Contents

How Do You Define Success?

When asked in an interview how it felt to be a big success, academy award-winning actor Ralph Feinnes answered:

> "Success? Well, I don't know quite what you mean by success. Material success? Worldly success? Personal, emotional success? The people I consider successful are so because of how they handle their responsibilities to other people, how they approach the future, people who have a full sense of the value of their life and what they want to do with it. I call people successful' not because they have money or their business is doing will but because, as human beings, they have a fully developed sense of being alive and engaged in a lifetime task of collaboration with other human beings—their mothers and fathers, their family, their friends, their loved ones, the friends who are dying, the friends who are being born."

How do you define success? Is it getting good grades? Having lots of friends? Making a particular athletic team? Owning your own car? Getting accepted by the college of your choice?

No matter what your vision of success, the exercises in this book will help you achieve it. That's because the personal qualities and skills that make people successful have been the subject of intense study and are quite well known. If you develop and nurture those qualities and life-skills in yourself, you can be successful at practically anything you set your mind to.

How to Use This Book

Think of this handbook as your own private journal. You'll get a lot more out of each exercise by being as honest with yourself as you can possibly be. Really think about the questions and take your time with the writing.

If a teacher or counselor gave you this book, he or she may ask that you share some of the things you've written during class or a group meeting. Take advantage of this opportunity whenever you can—chances are you'll learn a great deal more by interacting with your peers about the various topics. At the same time, remember that sharing is always voluntary. If you want to keep a piece of information private, by all means do so.

The exercises are grouped according to several themes. Read the information at the beginning of each section to find out a little about each one. If you are proceeding on your own, a good place to start is at the beginning of the book. Work through the exercises, page by page, at whatever speed feels comfortable. If you skip around in the book (which is okay, too) be sure to complete the exercises in each section in the order they are presented. Otherwise, you might miss and important concept or piece of information.

Intrapersonal Skills

Intra means *inside*. Intrapersonal skills are the skills you use to understand, communicate with, and control *yourself*. One of the most important tasks as a teenager is to get to know yourself. For example, it helps to know:

—what you can do well and not so well

—skills and talents that you can contribute

—your likes and dislikes

—feelings and thoughts you have about specific people, places and things

—what makes you feel happy, sad, worried, and angry

—what you believe in and consider important

By knowing these things about yourself, you are better able to influence and direct your own actions. In this first section, you'll take a look at such things as your feelings, thoughts, behaviors, values, and accomplishments. See how much you can learn about you!

Make Your Feelings Work For You!

Our feelings help us function in many ways. For example, have you ever become frightened and, because of your fear, done something to protect yourself from a real danger? If so, your feelings caused you to take positive action.

Below is a list of feeling words. Pick one or two of them, and see if you can briefly explain how that emotion affects your behavior. How does it work for you?

anger	joy	power	patience
eagerness	indecisiveness	satisfaction	love
fatigue	protectiveness	pain	hope
courage	silliness	curiosity	

_____

_____

Now take a moment to think about the emotions of self-pity, greed, jealousy, and possessiveness. **In what ways do you think those feelings affect behavior? What kinds of problems can they cause?**

_____

_____

Feelings have an effect on your body. They can wound and they can heal. Feelings can get "locked in" to your body when you refuse to accept and deal with them. This is a type of stress, and when it happens, real sickness can result. **Do you remember a time when you or someone else got sick under pressure? How about a stomachache or headache just before a test?**

Sometimes feelings show in the form of a twitch or tic in a muscle; other times as a tight jaw or lost voice. **Below is a list of body reactions. Next to each one, list feelings that you think can lead to these body reactions.**

Tears —————————————————————————————————

Smile —————————————————————————————————

Lump in throat ————————————————————————————

Pounding heart ————————————————————————————

Sweaty palms—————————————————————————————

Clenched fists —————————————————————————————

Shaky arms and legs————————————————————————

Bouncy walk ——————————————————————————————

Red face ————————————————————————————————

Tight stomach —————————————————————————————

Frown ——————————————————————————————

Squeaky voice ———————————————————————

Slouched posture ————————————————————

Here are some things to try:

Get rid of old guilt feelings you may still have about something you did. The best way might be to go to the person or people you wronged, admit it, and apologize. If that isn't possible, imagine the situation. Replay it in your mind, doing what you wish you had done the first time.

Affirm yourself. People tend to like people who like themselves. You might feel ridiculous doing this, but give it a try anyway. Look in the mirror and say the nicest things you can think of to yourself *in a sincere way*. Establish a relationship with yourself as your very best friend, the person you can always count on to be on *your* side.

Choose How You Feel!

You probably have things about yourself that you wish you could change. Some of those traits or characteristics *can* be changed—and some *can't*. But even if a trait cannot be changed, you don't have to feel miserable or depressed about it. Remember, negative feelings are caused by negative thoughts. The easiest way to stop feeling bad about a trait or characteristic is to change your thoughts about it.

So, instead of feeling embarrassed, self-conscious, or depressed about a trait, choose to do one of two things:

1. Change (or minimize) the trait.

2. Change your thoughts about the trait.

What could you do in each of these situations. Write down your ideas:

1. You dislike the color of your hair and think it makes you look drab.

   _____

   _____

   _____

   _____

2. You are very short, and think that short people have to fight for attention and respect.

   _____

   _____

   _____

   _____

3. The medication you are taking makes your face round and full. You think you look fat and ugly.

   _____

   _____

   _____

   _____

4. You have a hard time talking with people you don't know well. You feel shy and embarrassed when you meet new people and feel like you don't have anything interesting to say.

   _____

   _____

   _____

   _____

5. You think you are awkward and uncoordinated.

_____

_____

_____

_____

8. You hate your nose.

_____

_____

_____

_____

6. You think your feet are too big.

_____

_____

_____

_____

7. You use a wheelchair and think everyone feels sorry for you, which causes you to feel resentful.

_____

_____

_____

_____

9. You have a speech impediment and think it's not worth it to try to communicate with people.

_____

_____

_____

_____

10. You are self-conscious about your freckles.

_____

_____

_____

_____

What Do You Say When You Talk To Yourself?

Self-Assessment

Which kind of self-talk do you mostly engage in, positive or negative? Take this quiz and find out. **Circle the answer that sounds most like the way you talk to yourself.**

1. You enter a swimming competition. You do your best, but you don't win. What do you say to yourself?

    a. *If I had only tried harder, I'd have done better.*

    b. *I did the best I could and next time I'll do better.*

2. You run for student body president, but don't win. What do you say?

    a. *I'm a loser; I never get chosen for anything.*

    b. *I did the best I could and next time I'll do even better.*

3. You have a day when everything just seems to go wrong. You tell yourself:

    a. *I really messed up everything today.*

    b. *Everybody has days like this sometimes, and I'm just not going to let it get me down.*

4. You put off doing a task you don't like until the last minute and now you're faced with a deadline. Which do you say?

    a. *I'm so lazy. I never do anything until the last minute.*

    b. *I'm getting better about not leaving things until the last minute. The next time I do this I'll have more time.*

5. You're about to take a test in your most difficult subject. What do you say?

    a. *I'm really dumb in this subject; I'm never going to pass this test.*

    b. *I've really studied for this test. I'm confident that I'll do well.*

Try this:

*   For the next 3 days, pay close attention to your self-talk. Keep track of how frequently you use negative and positive self-talk.

*   Make a conscious effort to use positive self-talk more often.

*   Pay attention to the self-talk of the people around you.

*   Tell others how they can use positive self-talk.

Getting a Handle on Hostility

Anger is a normal but difficult emotion. Our anger often comes up in response to some other feeling — like hurt, worry, embarrassment, jealousy, or frustration. Knowing the feeling that *caused* our anger can make the anger itself easier to control. Read the situations below and see if you can empathize with Mark, Jennifer, and Sam enough to understand the emotions that *led to* their anger. Then brainstorm five alternative behaviors that would have achieved better results in each situation.

Situation 1: During a varsity baseball game, Mark ignores the base coach's signal and races for third base. As he slides into base the umpire calls him out. Mark immediately argues and makes rude remarks about the umpire's ability to see and judge the play. He continues his remarks as he moves toward the dugout. He kicks dirt, says things to the opposing team, and makes a gesture to the umpire who then kicks him out of the game. After he leaves the field, he shouts more angry remarks.

What were Mark's first feelings after he realized his mistake?

How could he have expressed those feelings in a more constructive way?

1. _____

_____

_____

2. _____

_____

_____

3. _____

_____

_____

Situation 2: Jennifer works at a fast food restaurant. She does not like working the drive-thru window but is often assigned that task. Two of her responsibilities are to ask the customers if they want drinks with their order and to offer new items on the menu. Jennifer tends to ignore that part of the job because the pressure is usually so intense that she can barely get the orders filled. Her manager has spoken to her before about the necessity of following these procedures. Today, Jennifer is more harried than usual and doesn't offer the new items or ask about drinks. On her break, the manager talks to her and tells her she must improve in this area or she will be fired. Jennifer glares at the manager, tenses her body, and grumbles, "If they want it, they'll order it. I shouldn't have to ask." The manager says it is part of the job. Jennifer cries, "You're never satisfied. I can't do anything right. I quit!"

What were Jennifer's first feelings when her manager confronted her?

How could she have expressed those feelings in a more constructive way?

1._____

_____

2._____

_____

3._____

_____

Situation 3: At home, Sam has been told repeatedly to clean his room. Frankly, it's become such a terrible mess that he doesn't know where to start. Besides, part of the reason it's a mess is that his older brother, who has gone off to college, is still taking up half the closet space. Today his mother has insisted that he will not go out with his friends again until his room is clean. Sam slams his bedroom door hard, takes a kick at the door leaving black scuff marks on it, and then makes a fist and punches a major hole in the wall. He lies down, lights up a cigarette, and plans how he will wait until his mother is busy and then go out to meet his friends anyway.

What were Sam's first feelings after his mother threatened to ground him?

How could he have expressed those feelings in a more constructive way?

1._____

_____

_____

2._____

_____

_____

3._____

_____

_____

Success Inventory

Your life is a chronicle of successes, one after another, year after year. The things you've accomplished could fill a book. Look back now at the child you were and the young adult you have become. Recall some of the many things you've learned and achieved, and write the most memorable here:

Five skills I mastered before the age of 5 were:

1. _____

2. _____

3. _____

4. _____

5. _____

Four things I accomplished between the ages of 5 and 8 were:

1. _____

2. _____

3. _____

4. _____

Four of my achievements between the ages of 8 and 11 were:

1. _____

_____

2. _____

_____

3. _____

_____

4. _____

_____

Three major things I accomplished between the ages of 11 and 13 were:

1. _____

_____

2. _____

_____

3. _____

_____

✳ ✳ ✳

Three of my successes between the age of 13 and now are:

1. _____

_____

2. _____

_____

3. _____

_____

Who Am I?

An important element of successful living is knowing "who you are." In order to develop a life that is meaningful, productive, and satisfying you need an accurate sense of self-understanding. You need to know your strengths and limitations, likes and dislikes, wants and needs, beliefs and values. The following questions will help you clarify these areas:

Think back to some of the things you've learned to do in life. The following questions will get you started:

What are some things you've learned quickly and easily? (List at least five. These don't have to be school subjects.)

1. _____

2. _____

3. _____

4. _____

5. _____

What is something that was hard to learn, that you mastered because you kept working at it?

_____

_____

What are some things you've been able to show other people how to do?

_____

_____

What are your major talents (strengths, abilities)?

_____

_____

What are some of your major accomplishments?

_____

_____

In what school subjects or activities are you most successful?

_____

_____

What about weaknesses?

First of all, everybody's got 'em. You aren't alone. Now that you've looked at some of your strengths, let's turn the coin over and look at some of the things that students say they sometimes have trouble with. If any of these apply to you, just put a ✔ next to the item:

____ 1. Using my time well
____ 2. Standing up for myself in a situation in which I know I am right
____ 3. Overcoming shyness
____ 4. Building self-confidence
____ 5. Giving myself credit for past achievements
____ 6. Giving myself credit for present strengths
____ 7. Learning from my mistakes
____ 8. Acknowledging my present weaknesses
____ 9. Starting a conversation with a member of the opposite sex

Examine yourself closely, and complete as many of the following items as you can:

My personal strengths (talents, skills, knowledge, accomplishments, favorite activities, etc.):	My personal weaknesses (handicaps, difficulties, limitations, things I don't know how to do yet, etc.):
1. _____	1. _____
2. _____	2. _____
3. _____	3. _____
4. _____	4. _____
5. _____	5. _____

If you are having trouble doing this, look more closely at what has happened to you during the past week or so.

What event or activity was a high point for you?

_____

_____

What was a low point?

_____

_____

Name one person you really enjoy being with:

_____

Describe something you've experienced lately (not necessarily last week) that you hope will never happen again:

_____

_____

Look back at what you've written. If you spot any clues to strengths and weaknesses you haven't thought of before, add them to your lists.

Now, complete the following half-sentences. Don't worry about being scrupulously honest or making perfect sense. Just have a good time looking at you.

I am a person who...

_____

Something I wish others could know about me is...

_____

_____

One of the things I feel proud of is...

_____

It's hard for me to admit that...

_____

One of the nicest things I could say about myself right now is...

_____

_____

A thing I accept in myself is...

_____

A thing I can't accept in others is...

_____

One thing that makes me angry is...

_____

The best thing about being a child was...

_____

a difficult thing about being a male/a female is...

_____

A good thing about being male/female is...

_____

The way I most need to improve is...

_____

When I feel my own energy flowing through me, I...

_____

When I give myself the right to enjoy life, I...

_____

One of the things I truly like and respect about myself is...

_____

I am happy when...

_____

I become angry when...

_____

I am sad when...

_____

I am fearful when...

_____

I feel lonely when...

_____

I have peace of mind when...

_____

I become frustrated when...

_____

I hate it when...

_____

I love it when...

_____

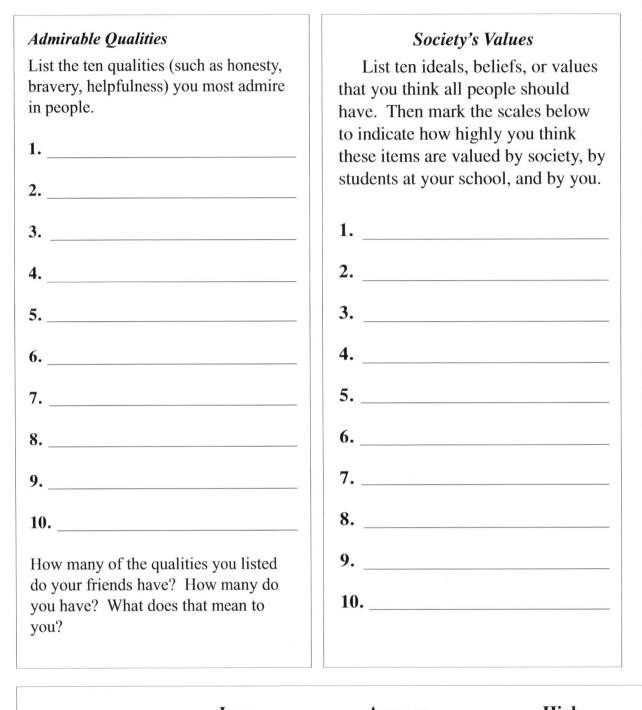

Admirable Qualities

List the ten qualities (such as honesty, bravery, helpfulness) you most admire in people.

1. _____

2. _____

3. _____

4. _____

5. _____

6. _____

7. _____

8. _____

9. _____

10. _____

How many of the qualities you listed do your friends have? How many do you have? What does that mean to you?

Society's Values

List ten ideals, beliefs, or values that you think all people should have. Then mark the scales below to indicate how highly you think these items are valued by society, by students at your school, and by you.

1. _____

2. _____

3. _____

4. _____

5. _____

6. _____

7. _____

8. _____

9. _____

10. _____

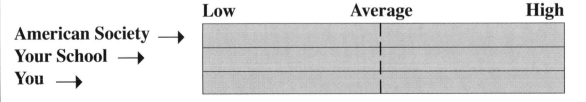

	Low	Average	High
American Society →			
Your School →			
You →			

Stop and think about how you are expressing your values the next time you express an opinion, choose a movie or TV program, or buy something.

How Do You Spend Your Time?

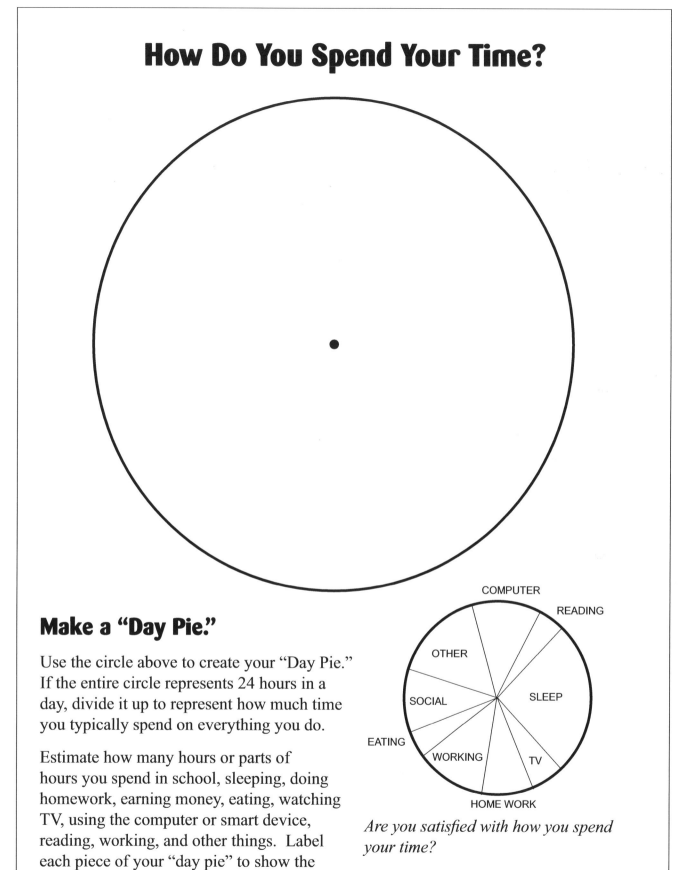

Make a "Day Pie."

Use the circle above to create your "Day Pie." If the entire circle represents 24 hours in a day, divide it up to represent how much time you typically spend on everything you do.

Estimate how many hours or parts of hours you spend in school, sleeping, doing homework, earning money, eating, watching TV, using the computer or smart device, reading, working, and other things. Label each piece of your "day pie" to show the major activity it represents. Once you've completed the pie, take a good look at it.

Are you satisfied with how you spend your time?

Where can you fit in the things that are most important to you?

Control Time-Wasters.

It has been said that, "You waste your time whenever you spend it doing something less important when you could be doing something more important." *Do you agree with that statement? Why or why not?*

To determine whether or not an activity is a time-waster for you, measure it against your goals. Is the activity helping you reach your goals? If not, how can you reduce or eliminate the time you devote to it?

Put a ✔ beside your time-wasters.

___**Telephone.** If you are frequently interrupted by phone calls while studying or working on an important project, try asking your friends to call you at an agreed-upon hour. Set aside a special time each day to make outgoing calls, too. Limit each call to a few minutes.

___**Television.** It's okay to watch your favorite shows, but don't watch TV just to fill (or kill) time. Instead, use that time to do something that will move you in the direction of a goal!

___**Cluttered room, work area, or desk.** How much time do you waste looking for misplaced items? Not very many people can do their best work amid disorganization. Take some time to "shape up" your space. Have at hand all necessary tools and materials. For studying, you'll need such things as books, paper, pens, pencils, calculator, notebooks, notes, erasers, dictionary, software, and any assistive devices you use.

___**Socializing.** Being with friends is important, but try not to let socializing distract you from other things that you've decided to do. When you plan your day, allow ample time for enjoyable interaction with friends and family. Then, when it's time to work on other goals, don't socialize.

___**Poor communication.** If you frequently fail to understand your assignments, misinterpret statements made by friends or family, or have trouble getting your own ideas across, put some extra effort into communicating effectively. Over 90 percent of all communication is spoken. That means you need to 1) state your own thoughts accurately and clearly, and 2) listen actively and attentively. Phrase your ideas in two or three different ways until you are certain others understand them. When listening, paraphrase what you've heard (restate it in your own words) or ask questions to ensure understanding.

___**Lack of planning.** Always write down your goals, assignments, appointments, chores, and job schedule. Then work out a weekly plan and follow it. With a plan, you'll never have to waste time wondering what to do next.

___**Poor study habits.** Here are some tips: Study at a desk or table. List your assignments in the order in which you plan to do them. Complete your most difficult assignments first while you are alert. Study without interruptions (phone calls) and distractions (TV or radio). Take frequent short breaks. As you read, write down questions that cross your mind. Ask those questions in class or discuss them with a friend. Periodically study with a classmate. Complete reading assignments before they are discussed in class.

___ **Procrastination.** Most of us tend to put off things that are unpleasant, things that are difficult, and things that involve tough decisions. These are often the very things that contribute most to our success! Try these procrastination cures:

- Do unpleasant tasks first. Or do them in small pieces, setting a deadline for each.

- Break down difficult tasks into smaller parts. Keep breaking down the parts until you see the first step.

- Break down difficult tasks into "mini jobs." Make each mini job small enough to finish in less than 10 minutes.

- Get more information. A task may seem difficult simply because you don't know enough about it. The more you know, the more likely you are to become interested and involved.

What' Your Attitude?

Your attitude is an expression of your thoughts and feelings. Your parents, teachers and friends will probably think you have a good attitude if you are eager to try new tasks, work hard without supervision, stick with hard tasks, are cheerful, friendly, accept responsibility, and obey rules. Sounds like a tall order, but since we all have control over how we express ourselves through our words and actions, we can decide if we want to be known for our good attitude or our bad attitude.

What was your attitude today?

_____

_____

_____

How did you show your attitude?

_____

_____

_____

Tips for Maintaining A Positive Attitude

✔ Be enthusiastic. Show that you appreciate being with the people you are with.

✔ Treat every person you meet as though he or she is the most important person you'll meet all day. If this feels awkward at first, do it anyway. Pretty soon, people will become truly important to you, and the awkwardness will go away.

✔ Develop a strong handshake. Then, while you're shaking hands, think a positive thought. For example: "This seems like a person I could learn a lot from. I'd really like to know this person better."

✔ Act like someone who gets the job done. Don't say, "I'll try." It sounds uncertain. Instead say, "I will" or "I'll have an answer for you by five." (Then make sure that you do!)

✔ Focusing on the positive can help you maintain a positive attitude. How can you do your best if you only see the worst? Whatever you're involved with focus on the positive parts. Work to change the negative parts. If they can't be changed, accept them.

Even though attitudes are inside, they usually show. That's because we express our attitudes by the things we say and do. We express them through our words and our faces. They show in our energy level and in the choices we make.

Think of a time when you *strongly disliked* a person's attitude. See if you can describe how that person came across. You might get some ideas by looking at the list of words, at the bottom of the page.

_____

_____

_____

_____

_____

Now, think of a time when you *liked* or *admired* a person's attitude. Again, see if any words on the list below describe how the person came across.

_____

_____

_____

_____

_____

arrogant	confident	afraid	bossy
sullen	interested	wimpy	critical
angry	kind	cheerful	reluctant
argumentative	responsible	eager	complaining
defensive	helpful	adventurous	careless
bored	humble	industrious	whiny

Interpersonal Skills

Inter means *between*. Interpersonal skills are the skills you use to interact effectively with others —to observe, communicate, cooperate, and get things done.

One very important interpersonal skill is listening. Through listening, you gather information, get to know others, and build trust. In addition, listening also helps you lead discussions, work out agreements, and settle conflicts. Of course, you also have to be able to get your own ideas across. Words and actions help you express thoughts and get your ideas across.

Another interpersonal skill is the ability to observe others and understand some of the things they are *not* saying — like feelings or thoughts they might be hesitant to express. People communicate a great deal by how they sit, stand, and walk, and by their tone of voice and facial expressions. This way of communicating is called *body language*. Successful people pay careful attention to body language.

What Blocks Communication?

Have you ever tried to have a conversation with someone who wouldn't let you finish a sentence? Have you ever attempted to discuss a problem with someone who had an answer for everything? Read through this list of communication blockers. Think about how you feel when someone throws one of them your way. More importantly, try to be aware of any that you may use. Being aware of poor communication habits is the first step in improving those habits.

Interrupting

Interruptions are the most common cause of stalled communication. It's frustrating to be interrupted in the middle of a sentence, and when interruptions happen over and over again, talking begins to feel like a waste of time.

Do you do this? (Mark with a ✔)

___ Never

___ Occasionally

___ More often than I should

___ A lot

Advising

Few people enjoy getting unasked-for advice. Statements that begin with, "Well, if I were you...," or "If you ask me...," are like red flags. Advice-giving says, "I'm superior. I know better than you do." Advice can also cause a person to feel powerless—as though she can't make a good decision on her own.

Do you do this? (Mark with a ✔)

___ Never

___ Occasionally

___ More often than I should

___ A lot

Judging

When you tell people that their ideas or feelings are wrong, you are saying in effect that you know more than they do. If your ideas are drastically different from theirs, they'll either defend themselves (argue) or give up on the conversation. Even positive judgments like, "You're the smartest student in class," don't work if the person you're talking to doesn't *feel* very smart.

Do you do this? (Mark with a ✔)

___ Never

___ Occasionally

___ More often than I should

___ A lot

Interpreting

Some people develop a habit of analyzing everything (including statements) to reveal "deeper meanings." When you interpret or analyze, you imply an unwillingness to accept the speaker or the speaker's statements just as they are. Analyzing is for psychiatrists and counselors, and a lot of the time even *they* are wrong!

Do you do this? (Mark with a ✔)

___ Never

___ Occasionally

___ More often than I should

___ A lot

Dominating

We all know how frustrating and annoying it is to be in a conversation with someone who always has something better and more interesting to say than we do. In addition, when you dominate a conversation, others are forced to use another communication stopper, *interrupting*, just to get a word in.

Do you do this? (Mark with a ✔)

___ Never

___ Occasionally

___ More often than I should

___ A lot

Probing

Asking a lot of questions ("Why did you go there?" "Who did you see?" "What did he do?") tends to put the speaker on the defensive by requiring her to explain every statement. More importantly, your questions may lead the speaker *away from* what she originally wanted to say. If you ask too many questions, you are controlling, not sharing, the conversation.

Do you do this? (Mark with a ✔)

___ Never

___ Occasionally

___ More often than I should

___ A lot

Challenging/Accusing/Contradicting

There's nothing more frustrating than trying to talk with someone who challenges everything you say, insists that your ideas are wrong, or states that what happened was your fault. Contradictions and accusations put the speaker on the spot, and make the speaker defensive.

Do you do this? (Mark with a ✔)

___ Never

___ Occasionally

___ More often than I should

___ A lot

Criticizing/Name-calling/Put-downs

Don't make sarcastic or negative remarks in response to the things someone says. Criticism whittles away at self-esteem. Hardly anyone wants to continue a conversation that's making him feel bad or small. Even name-calling and put-downs that sound funny can still be hurtful. In the long run, they damage friendships.

Do you do this? (Mark with a ✔)

___ Never

___ Occasionally

___ More often than I should

___ A lot

Look back over the items you checked and decide where you could make some improvements. List them here:

_____

_____

_____

_____

_____

_____

_____

_____

Make a commitment to yourself to pay attetion to changing these poor communication habits and practice new habits every time you're in a conversation

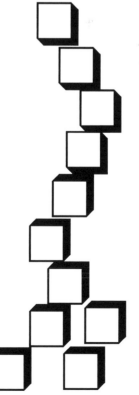

Being A Good Listener

Listening is a very important part of good communication and is a skill that can be learned. When you are talking with someone, practice the characteristics of a good listener—that's how you become one!

People generally like to spend time with others who are good listeners. Learning to be a good listener will help you in all aspects of your life from your social life to your career.

Listed below are characteristics of a good listener.
Check ones that describe you most of the time.

HEARING CHECK UP!

A good listener:

____ Faces the speaker.

____ Looks into the speaker's eyes.

____ Is relaxed, but attentive.

____ Keeps an open mind.

____ Listens to the words and tries to picture what the speaker is saying.

____ Doesn't interrupt or fidget.

____ Waits for the speaker to pause to ask clarifying questions.

____ Tries to feel what the speaker is feeling (shows empathy).

____ Nods and says "uh huh," or summarizes to let the speaker know he/she is listening.

What is your strongest quality as a listener?

_____

_____

What is your weakest quality as a listener?

_____

_____

How can you become a better listener?

_____

_____

Practicing "I" Statements

When another person does something we don't like, we may be tempted to send the person a **"you" message**. "You" messages tend to be blaming messages. They can make the other person feel mad or hurt—and they often make the situation worse.

Try using an **"I" message** instead. "I" messages talk about your feelings and needs. They can help the other person understand you without blaming him or her for the problem. Here's how to make an "I" message:

1. **Describe the situation.**

   "When my bike gets left out in the rain…"

2. **Say how you feel.**

   "I get upset because it will be damaged."

3. **Describe what you want the person to do.**

   "When my bike gets left out in the rain, I get upset because it will be damaged. I would really appreciate it if you would put it inside after you ride it."

Now, you try it! Read the "you" message in the first cartoon bubble. Then write a better message—an "I" message—in the second bubble.

You sneak! You took my bike without asking. If you ever touch it again, I'll knock your head off!

When _____ ,

I feel _____ ,

_____ *and I want you to* _____

_____

_____

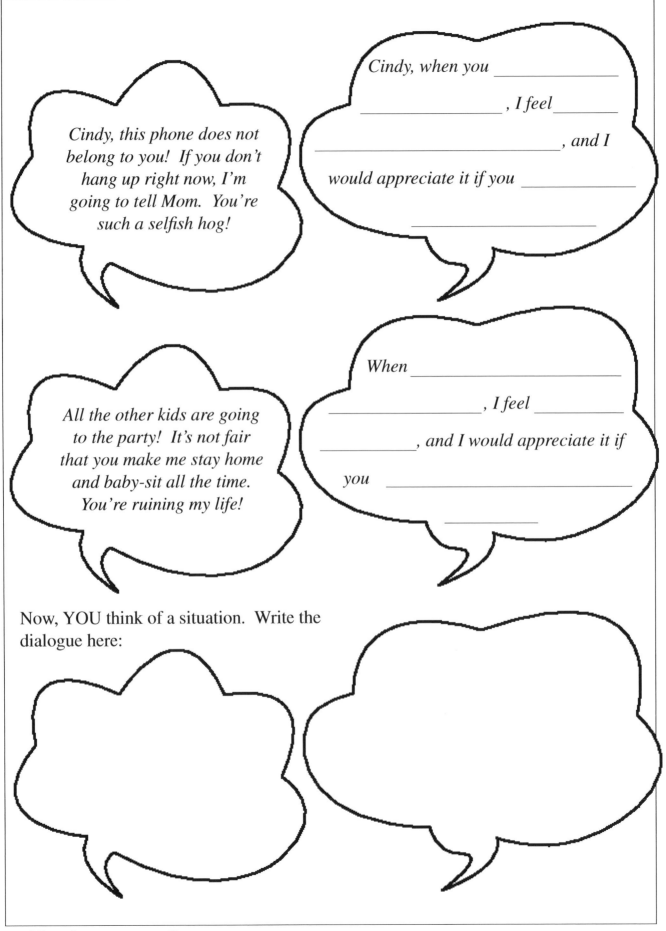

Cindy, this phone does not belong to you! If you don't hang up right now, I'm going to tell Mom. You're such a selfish hog!

Cindy, when you _____ _____, I feel _____ _____, and I would appreciate it if you _____ _____

All the other kids are going to the party! It's not fair that you make me stay home and baby-sit all the time. You're ruining my life!

When _____ _____, I feel _____ _____, and I would appreciate it if you _____ _____

Now, YOU think of a situation. Write the dialogue here:

Body Talk
Words Are Only Part of Communication

You also communicate with your body all the time. As you react emotionally to events in your life, your body takes on different postures, positions, and facial expressions.

How do people express the following emotions through their body language? What do they do with their bodies? How would they look to others? Describe the body language you would observe below:

Embarrassment: _____

_____

Nervousness: _____

_____

Excitement: _____

_____

Boredom: _____

_____

Anger: _____

_____

Fear: _____

_____

Happiness: _____

_____

> **When you are talking with someone, be aware of the message you are giving with your body language. Does it reinforce your words or is your body saying something different?**

Friendship

Successful people usually enjoy positive, fulfilling relationships with others. They know how to make and keep friends. By managing your life in a responsible, positive way, you earn the respect, admiration, and friendship of others. And as you build a network of friends, your opportunities for success will increase. More people listen to your ideas, turn to you for advice and assistance, and willingly join in activities that you think are important.

So this handbook helps you work on your friendship skills. Learn how to meet people. Find ways to show your current friends how much you appreciate them. Renew an old friendship and strengthen a new one.

What Is a Friend?

1. ____YES ___NO   A friend is someone who knows all about me and likes me as I am.

2. ____YES ___NO   To be my friend, a person must agree with me on just about every subject or issue.

3. ____YES ___NO   A friend is someone who doesn't care how much money I have.

4. ____YES ___NO   To be my friend, a person must have the same racial, cultural, and religious background as I.

5. ____YES ___NO   A friend is someone who'll do whatever I say.

6. ____YES ___NO   A friend is someone who listens to me even if I am talking about my troubles.

7. ____YES ___NO   To be my friend, a person must demonstrate respect for me.

If you said "YES" to numbers 1, 3, 6, and 7, you have probably had some real friends. Your friends know and like you because of the person you are, which includes the color or your skin, the way you speak, how much money you have, your abilities, and your disabilities. They care how you feel. They listen to your thoughts and feelings. That's how they prove that they are friends. If you answered "NO" to numbers 2, 4, and 5, you realize that everybody's different and that's great. Friends don't have to look alike, talk the same way, come from the same background, or agree with each other all of the time. And they don't always have to do what each other wants to prove their friendship.

Think of a friend you had when you were a child:

What did you like about your friend?

_____

_____

What do you think he or she liked about you?

_____

_____

What was one of the best times you ever had together?

_____

_____

Think about someone who is your friend now:

How did your friendship begin?

_____

_____

_____

_____

What are some things you like to do together?

_____

_____

_____

_____

How is your friendship different now from the way if was in the beginning?

_____

_____

_____

_____

Have you ever had a friendship that seemed bad for you? What was it about that friendship that was negative?

_____

_____

_____

`_____

_____

List the most important things you want in a friend.

1. _____

_____

2. _____

_____

3. _____

_____

4. _____

_____

5. _____

_____

6. _____

_____

Other things to think about:

What do you think you would do if you wanted to be friends with someone who spoke a different language?

What do you think you'd do if a friend of yours started doing something you thought was wrong or dangerous?

How could you make friends with someone who is blind?
... someone who is deaf?

Becoming a Better Friend

Friends are important! If you could take three people with you on a trip around the world, whom would you take? Why?

Name	Reason
1.	
2.	
3.	

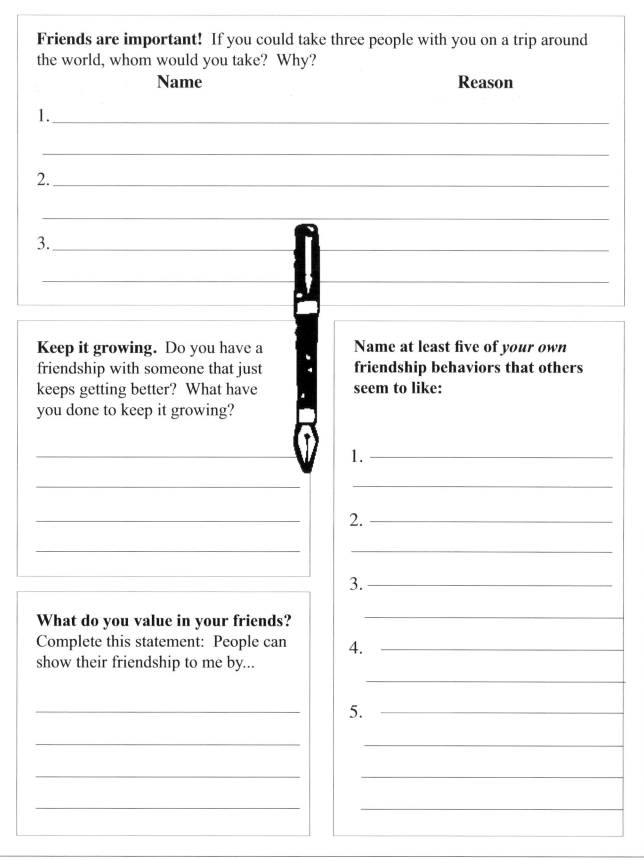

Keep it growing. Do you have a friendship with someone that just keeps getting better? What have you done to keep it growing?

Name at least five of *your own* friendship behaviors that others seem to like:

1.

2.

3.

4.

5.

What do you value in your friends? Complete this statement: People can show their friendship to me by...

Name two of *your own* friendship behaviors that seem to turn others off:

1._____

_____

2._____

_____

Think of *one way* in which you would like to improve your friendship behavior. Write a GOAL here:

_____

_____

_____

_____

_____

_____

_____

To achieve your goal, you need a PLAN—a systematic way of putting your goal into action. What are some of the first steps you can take?

Step 1:_____

_____

Step 2:_____

_____

Step 3:_____

_____

Step 4:_____

_____

Step 5:_____

_____

Step 6: _____

_____

_____

Don't walk in front of me—
I may not follow.
Don't walk behind me—
I may not lead.
Walk beside me—
and just be my friend.

—Camus

A Friendship Problem

Sometimes friends do things that upset us. Think of a time when there was a problem between you and a friend. What happened? What did your friend do? What did you do?

Describe the problem here:

_____

_____

Did the problem get resolved? _____

Why or why not?

_____

_____

If the problem isn't resolved, what can you do now to make it better?

_____

_____

Remember this—All problems and conflicts between people have at least two points of view. You described your point of view above. Take some time and really think about where your friend is coming from.

Describe your friends point of view here:

_____

_____

When you consider your friends point of view, how does it help you come up with a strategy that you can use to resolve the problem or prevent similar problems in the future?

_____

_____

What advice would you give to someone about solving friendship problems?

_____

_____

Health & Fitness

One of the things that can seriously interfere with your success is letting yourself get into a weakened physical or mental state. The responsibilities of school, family, extra curricular activities and work (if you have a job) demand that you be in the best condition possible.

Don't confuse hard work — without regard for personal well-being —with success. Success takes more than drive and talent. To be successful, you must keep yourself healthy and fit so that you can handle all of the demands facing you.

Here's a useful comparison: Think about a logger cutting trees in the forest. It not only takes skill to bring down trees safely and efficiently, it takes the right tools. The logger must occasionally stop cutting trees to sharpen his or her saw. Similarly, you must occasionally take breaks to renew yourself and your skills. When you fail to "sharpen the saw," you have to use more and more effort to accomplish the same tasks. Eventually you may be unable to perform at all. Without regular maintenance, dullness happens.

The activities in this section focuses on some of the most important ingredients in wellness and fitness. One is the management of stress. Others are diet and exercise.

Health Inventory
Self-Assessment

Think about what you do to take care of yourself. Circle one number for each statement. Circle 5 if the statement describes you perfectly, 4 if it is mostly true, 3 if it is somewhat true, 2 if it is mostly untrue, and 1 if it is not at all true.

Circle One	Read Carefully	+ / -	Circle One	Read Carefully	+ / -
1 2 3 4 5	I eat a balanced diet.		1 2 3 4 5	I often eat at fast food restaurants.	
1 2 3 4 5	My weight is about right for me.		1 2 3 4 5	I often stay up very late.	
1 2 3 4 5	I engage in a regular exercise program.		1 2 3 4 5	I tire easily.	
1 2 3 4 5	I have an abundance of energy.		1 2 3 4 5	I understand it takes good physical health to achieve other goals in life.	
1 2 3 4 5	I have specific goals related to physical fitness.		1 2 3 4 5	I am frequently sick.	
1 2 3 4 5	I get adequate rest.		1 2 3 4 5	I often experience tension in my family or social life.	
1 2 3 4 5	I sleep well at night.		1 2 3 4 5	I always fasten my seat belt.	
1 2 3 4 5	I have regular physical checkups.		1 2 3 4 5	I usually follow rules of safety.	
1 2 3 4 5	I often have indigestion.		1 2 3 4 5	I try to reduce sodium, fat, and sugar in my diet.	
1 2 3 4 5	I often eat fast.				

Now, in the right-hand column, put a + if you are pleased with your rating. Put a − if you would like to improve in the area described.

What general statements can you make about your health?_____

_____

_____

In what areas do you need to improve?_____

_____

_____

What is one thing you can start doing to make this improvement?_____

_____

_____

How Much Stress Are You Juggling?

Everyone experiences stress at times. Stress is a fact of life. You can't totally avoid it, but you can learn how to manage your response to stressful situations so you don't suffer the negative effects on your health and wellbeing. The first step in reducing stress is to become aware of the major sources of stress in your life

How much stress are you trying to juggle? Here's a way to find out:

1. Inside each ball the juggler is keeping in the air list a stressful situation, event, or problem that you've been dealing with lately. Since big positive events can also be stressful, be sure to include positive as well as negative events.

2. Near the juggler's body, write down all the **physical symptoms** that you experience in *your* body as a result of the stressors you are juggling.

3. In the space in the middle, write down the **external effects** these stressors are having on your life.

What did you learn about how you handle stress from this activity?

_____

_____

_____

_____

_____

_____

Stress and Me

When you are under too much stress — feeling tired, worried, pressured — you are more likely to experience health problems, memory loss, and learning difficulties. And it just plain doesn't feel good. Knowing ways to manage and reduce stress will minimize its destructive effects on your life and health.

Read this list of possible stressors and decide, on a scale of 1 to 5, how concerned you are about each one. Circle 1 on the scale if you never experience this kind of stress. Circle 5 on the scale if you experience this kind of stress frequently and in large doses.

1 2 3 4 5   **1. I am concerned about my grades.**

1 2 3 4 5   **2. I am concerned about disappointing my parents.**

1 2 3 4 5   **3. I am concerned about being lonely.**

1 2 3 4 5   **4. I am concerned about not fitting in at school.**

1 2 3 4 5   **5. I am concerned about making friends.**

1 2 3 4 5   **6. I am concerned about losing a friend.**

1 2 3 4 5   **7. I am concerned about being bullied.**

1 2 3 4 5   **8. I am concerned about being shy.**

1 2 3 4 5   **9. I am concerned about my health.**

1 2 3 4 5   **10. I am concerned about the health of a family member.**

1 2 3 4 5   **11. I am concerned about money.**

1 2 3 4 5   **12. I am concerned about my parents divorcing.**

1 2 3 4 5   **13. I am concerned about my weight.**

1 2 3 4 5   **14. I am concerned about my appearance.**

1 2 3 4 5   **15. I am concerned about dying.**

1 2 3 4 5   **16. I am concerned about a specific subject or teacher.**

1 2 3 4 5   **17. I am concerned about alcohol or drugs.**

1 2 3 4 5   **18. I am concerned about my safety.**

1 2 3 4 5   **19. I am concerned about responsibilities I have.**

1 2 3 4 5   **20. I am concerned about** _____

_____

My Stress Management Strategies

Here are some things that people do to manage stress effectively:

Put checks (✔) in front of the things you have tried.

_____ Deep breathing

_____ Listening to relaxing, soothing, or uplifting music

_____ Exercising

_____ Closing your eyes and thinking of a happy memory or something you're looking forward to doing.

_____ Laughing

_____ Taking a warm bath or shower

_____ Talking it over with a friend

_____ Playing a game or sport

Now list some things that you can start doing, or continue doing that will help you cope with the thing that is causing your stress.

_____

_____

_____

_____

_____

In what ways will doing these things have a positive impact on you?

_____

_____

_____

_____

Exercise and Fitness

Exercise is one of the simplest and most effective ways to reduce your stress and promote good health. Vigorous physical exertion is a natural way for your body to release stress and return to a normal, relaxed, and refreshed state.

Here are some facts you should know about physical exercise:

Cardiovascular Fitness: The ability of the heart and lungs to take in and use oxygen. Aerobic exercises increase and maintain cardiovascular fitness. Dancing, swimming, biking, rowing, jogging, and brisk walking are examples of aerobic exercise.

Muscular Strength: The ability of the muscles to apply or exert force. Weight training (or "lifting") builds and maintains muscle mass and strength.

Muscle Endurance: The ability of the muscles to continue an activity over a period of time without fatigue. Good endurance allows a person to exercise longer and is particularly helpful in activities such as long-distance walking or running, cross country skiing, soccer, and basketball.

Flexibility: The ability to move the muscles to their full extent, without strain. Flexible muscles are the best guard against muscle pulls and strains, and lower back injuries. Stretching should be a part of both the warm up and cool down phases of all fitness programs. Flexibility is of utmost importance in activities like gymnastics, karate, judo, and ballet.

What kinds of exercise do you enjoy? _____

_____

_____

How often do you exercise? _____

_____

Do you need to increase the amount of exercise you get? Yes, ____ No ____

What can you do to motivate yourself to exercise more? _____

_____

_____

My Wellness Plan

Develop a GOAL in each of the wellness areas listed below. A goal is something to shoot for—something to accomplish. Don't make your goals too hard, but don't make them too easy either. Challenge yourself enough to make each goal worth working for!

Brainstorm a list of things that might stand in the way of your accomplishing each goal. Then list the steps that you can take to overcome these barriers. Finally, list any other steps that you need to take to reach the goal.

FITNESS

Goal: _____

_____

Possible **barriers** to accomplishing the goal:

_____   _____

_____   _____

Steps to overcoming the barriers and achieving the goal:

❶ _____

❷ _____

❸ _____

❹ _____

❺ _____

PERSONAL HEALTH BEHAVIORS

Goal: _____

_____

Possible **barriers** to accomplishing the goal:

_____   _____

_____   _____

Steps to overcoming the barriers and achieving the goal:

➊ _____

➋ _____

➌ _____

➍ _____

➎ _____

NUTRITION

Goal: _____

_____

Possible **barriers** to accomplishing the goal:

_____   _____

_____   _____

Steps to overcoming the barriers and achieving the goal:

➊ _____

➋ _____

➌ _____

➍ _____

➎ _____

COPING WITH STRESS

Goal: _____

_____

Possible **barriers** to accomplishing the goal:

_____   _____

_____   _____

Steps to overcoming the barriers and achieving the goal:

❶ _____

❷ _____

❸ _____

❹ _____

❺ _____

AVOIDANCE OF RISKY BEHAVIORS

Goal: _____

_____

Possible **barriers** to accomplishing the goal:

_____   _____

_____   _____

Steps to overcoming the barriers and achieving the goal:

❶ _____

❷ _____

❸ _____

❹ _____

❺ _____

Nutrition Information

Good nutrition doesn't just happen. Your body needs a wide variety of vitamins, minerals and other nutrients to stay in top condition, and you have to make sure it gets them. Here are four steps you can take to stay in shape:

1. Drink plenty of water. All the parts of your body need water to function, plus water is the main ingredient in your body's cooling system.

2. Eat for energy. Choose a variety of foods, but concentrate on getting enough *complex carbohydrates*. These are the foods that come from the first two food groups listed below.

3. Limit fats, sugar, and salt. Ice cream, candy, potato chips, and other snack foods may taste good, but they don't provide many nutrients. If you had a luxury car, you wouldn't just fill it with cheap gas while forgetting about oil, lubricants, and all other forms of maintenance. Treat your body like a luxury car — give it the best possible care!

4. Eat frequent, small meals. Don't skip breakfast or pig out at dinner. Your "engine" needs fuel all day long, and it never likes to be flooded.

Ideal Servings Per Day

Number of Servings	Food Group	Serving Size Examples
4	vegetables/fruits	1/2 cup, or 1 apple, 1 orange 1 banana, medium potato
4	breads/cereals/pasta	1 slice bread, 3/4 cup cereal 1 tortilla
2-4	milk, cheese, yogurt	1 cup milk, 1 medium slice of cheese
2	meat, poultry, fish, eggs, beans, nuts	2-3 oz lean meat, poultry, fish, 2 eggs, 1 1/4 cup cooked beans, 4 tablespoons peanut butter, 3/4 cup nuts

Menu Planning

Plan all of your meals and snacks for one day. Include appropriate servings from each of the four food groups. You'll find that information on your "Nutrition Information" sheet.

	Meat/Beans	Fruits/Vegetables	Breads/Cereals	Milk/Cheese
Breakfast				
Snack				
Lunch				
Snack				
Dinner				
Snack				

Goal Setting

You may not realize it, but you set goals all the time. In fact, just about every task you accomplish is a goal before it becomes a reality. The process of goal setting is so natural that much of the time you don't even think about it.

Just imagine how much more you could get done if you spent some time thinking about your goals each day — wide awake and very deliberately.

To be truly successful you *must* think about goals. Why? Because that's basically what success is — managing your life to achieve an ongoing series of goals, like graduation, acceptance at the college of your choice, or landing an entry-level job in your chosen field. If you don't know what you want or where to go and how to get there, you won't even know how to measure success, let alone achieve it.

Who's in Charge of Your Life?

Without giving them a lot of thought, quickly answer these questions:

What do you want in life?

_____

_____

_____

What is one goal you have for yourself right now?

_____

_____

_____

Do you feel in charge of your life?

_____

_____

Are you happy with the direction your life seems to be taking?

_____

_____

Why or why not?

_____

_____

_____

Why is setting goals important? Because goals can help you do, be, and experience everything you want in life. Instead of just letting life happen to you, goals allow you to *make* your life happen.

Successful and happy people have a vision of how their life should be and they set lots of goals (both short term and long range) to help them reach their vision. A man named David Starr Jordan said, "The world stands aside to let anyone pass who knows where he is going." You can bet that those people who know where they are going are getting there by setting goals.

When you set goals, you are taking control of your life. It's like having a map to show you where you want to go. Think of it this way: You have two drivers. One driver has a destination (her goal) which is laid out for her on the map. She can drive straight there without any wasted time or wrong turns. The other driver has no goal or destination or map. He starts off at the same time from the same place as the first driver, but he drives aimlessly around, never getting anywhere, using up gas and oil. Which driver do you want to be like?

Winners in life set goals and follow through on them. Winners decide what they want in life and then get there by making plans and setting goals. Unsuccessful people just let life happen by accident. Which do you want to be? You do have a choice. Goals aren't difficult to set—and they aren't difficult to reach. You decide.

Do you remember some of the benefits of setting goals? Write down three:

1. _____

_____

_____

_____

2. _____

_____

_____

_____

3. _____

_____

_____

_____

Man with a Vision

GEORGE W. CARVER (1864-1943)

George Washington Carver was born into slavery. Shortly after his birth on a farm in Missouri, his father was run over by a wagon and killed. Before George was a year old, a band of night raiders kidnapped him and his mother. George was found, but not his mother.

Moses and Sue Carver kept George and gave him their name. They had no children of their own and raised George and his brother, Jim, as if they were their sons.

The Carvers were not educated people, yet both were aware of the unusual curiosity that George had about what made things grow; he wanted to know the name of every plant. He made himself a secret garden where he nursed sick plants back to health. Whenever the weather permitted, George spent his Sundays in the woods, studying the plant life.

Mrs. Carver got a speller for George, and he learned every word in it. He heard of a school for blacks that he wanted to attend, but it was in Neosha, eight miles away. He would have to live there. The Carvers were concerned about his survival, for he had no place to stay and no money for food; however, they knew how much learning meant to him, so they gave their consent. George was only ten years old, but he walked to Neosha with confidence. As soon as he got there, he met a black woman, Mariah Watkins, who offered him room and board in trade for work. As Mariah never had children of her own,

she treated George like a son. She taught him how to wash and iron, two skills that served him well in the years to come.

The school George entered was a cabin about fourteen feet wide and sixteen feet long. He had to fight for space with seventy-five other children. There was no high school in Neosha. When George was thirteen, he hitchhiked a ride in a covered wagon to Kansas, where he entered high school at Fort Scott. To support himself, he worked as a houseboy for the wealthiest family in town. Again he had a home, regular meals, and a bed at night.

George worked very hard at his studies. His short-term goal was to go to college, yet he knew he had to have a way to support himself. So he put to use all the skills he had learned about washing, ironing, and sewing, and he opened a laundry business!

George applied to Highland University in Kansas City. He received a letter from the University complimenting him on his fine grades and record of achievements. They said he could enroll in the fall. When he appeared for registration, the person in charge was surprised to find he was black, and would not permit George to register. He was devastated and heartbroken because he had set his heart on a college education. George began to wander across the western states, not knowing what to do.

He heard about homesteading in Kansas and decided to give it a try. He filed for 160 acres but had no tools to develop the claim and no money. When it was time to pay the taxes, he lost the land. He was twenty-five years old and still determined to get a college education.

Finally, George gained admittance to Simpson College in Iowa. He took in laundry and paid his way through Simpson College.

George studied art and liked to paint. When his art teacher became aware of his interest in plants, she wrote her brother who was a professor of horticulture at Iowa State College. George was admitted and became the first black to graduate from that institution.

George had some difficult times at Iowa State. Black students were not allowed in the dormitory, and he was not allowed to eat in the student dining hall. But he was very determined and would not allow himself to become discouraged. He was well liked by the students, and they included him in all activities. They made him feel that the color of his skin was unimportant.

George combined his love of plants and art by painting many still-life canvases and entering them at the Iowa Exhibit of State Artists. He won several prizes, and four of his paintings were exhibited at the World's Fair at Chicago.

George graduated in 1894 and remained two more years to attain his M.A. degree. He then became assistant instructor in botany in charge of the greenhouse. He no longer had to work as a laundryman, janitor, houseboy, or cook. George could spend all of his time on the campus and in his greenhouse. He was very happy, but he knew he must move on.

Offers of jobs came to George from a number of Southern Negro colleges. One of the offers was from Tuskegee. Booker T. Washington, the president, wanted George to head the Department of agriculture and teach natural sciences. He accepted the position. When asked why, he said, "It has always been the one great ideal of my life to be of the greatest good to the greatest number of my people possible. I took up agriculture because I feel that it is the key that will open the door of freedom for my people. Mr. Washington feels the same way."

When he reached Tuskegee, George was given a small laboratory of his own. From this laboratory came formulas in agricultural chemistry that enriched the Southland.

Tuskegee was situated in the cotton belt. Cotton had been planted on the same acres repeatedly until all the richness had been taken out of the soil. It was no longer a profitable crop. One of Tuskegee's tasks was to teach the farmers to raise other crops to save the land. George showed them the value of rotating crops. He introduced a variety of useful products derived from peanuts and sweet potatoes, two crops that grew easily in the Alabama soil. Out of his experiments with the peanut came a two-hundred million dollar industry.

Over the years, George W. Carver was awarded many honorary degrees. Private industry sought his services.

Thomas A. Edison offered him $50,000 a year to work in his laboratories. However, George turned down each of these offers, for he cared nothing about money and never applied for a patent on any of his discoveries. He used to say, "God gave them to me. Why should I claim to own them?"

George remained at Tuskegee the rest of his life. The year 1936-37 was dedicated to him. His fibers, paints, stains, and peanut and sweet potato products were on exhibit. There were 118 sweet potato products. Thirty-six of his paintings were displayed along with hundreds of his lace designs. There were wall paper designs and wall board, mats and rugs, and vases made from Alabama clays.

George rose from slavery to become a famous scientist, overcoming all obstacles, including those of racial discrimination.

(Adapted from Smile, You're Worth It!, by Margo Kluth and Dorothy McCarthy. Me and My Innerself, San Clemente, California, 1983.)

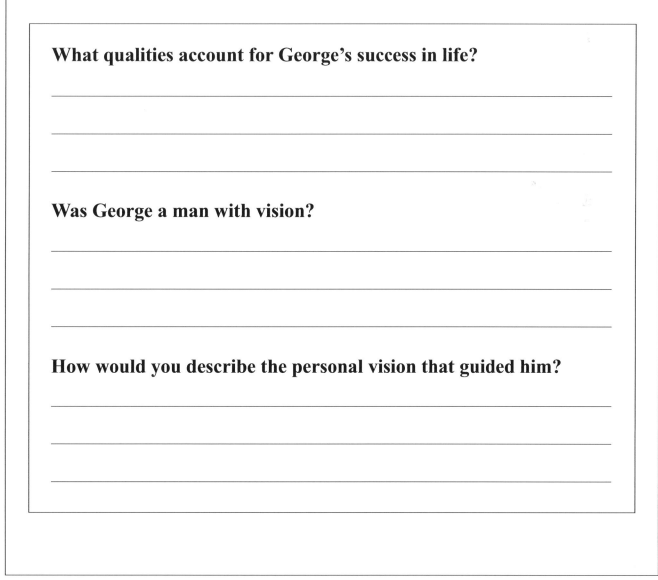

What qualities account for George's success in life?

_____

_____

_____

Was George a man with vision?

_____

_____

_____

How would you describe the personal vision that guided him?

_____

_____

_____

My Personal Vision

THE IMPORTANT THING IS NOT SO MUCH WHERE WE ARE —BUT IN WHAT DIRECTION WE ARE MOVING.

Think about the questions you answered in the experience sheet "Who's in Charge of Your Life?" and about what you have just learned about the power of personal vision from the story of George Washington Carver. Now put all of your learnings and reactions together, and develop some ideas about *your* personal vision. Remember, you are a unique individual and your vision and goals may be quite different from anyone else's. It's up to you to find out what your ideals and visions really are. You are the one who must decide what to pursue and in what direction to focus your efforts.

Three areas I am interested in are:

1. _____

2. _____

3. _____

Three important values I hold are:

1. _____

_____

2. _____

_____

3. _____

_____

A personal vision I have for my life is:

_____

_____

_____

_____

Tips for Setting Goals

1. *Goals must be clear and describe exactly what you want or will do.*

2. *Goals must be personal.* They must be about you, not someone else.

3. *Goals must be measurable.* You need to know when you have achieved your goal.

4. *Goals must have realistic time limits.*

5. *Goals must be manageable.* Divide big goals into several smaller, attainable goals or tasks. This will enable you to experience results in a shorter period to time.

6. *Goals must be stated in positive rather than negative terms*: (I *will* do something rather than I *won't* do something.)

7. *Goals must be written down.* People are more likely to achieve goals that are in writing. Written goals can be reviewed regularly, and have more power. Like a contract with yourself, they are harder to neglect or forget.

You Can Reach Your Goals!

What are goals?

A goal is an end, home base, the final destination, what you are aiming for. Goals can center on having something—clothes, a car, money—or they can center on achieving—finishing school, going to college, having a career, becoming famous, gaining knowledge and honors.

Short-term and long-range goals

Short-term goals include making phone calls, finishing your homework, cleaning your room, doing your chores, or making plans for the weekend. Long-range goals might include planning a trip for next summer, deciding to go to a trade school, a community college, or a university; saving money to buy something special; or making plans for your future career.

How to write a goal

When we write goals in the way described on the previous page, we connect with the part of our brain that tells us what we need to do. The more often you set goals in this way, the more often you get what you want.

Goals are broken down into steps

Have you ever wanted to make something? If you have, you may remember that after you decided what you wanted to make (this was your goal) you started thinking of things you needed to have and/or do in order to attain your goal. These are the steps necessary to take in order to achieve your goal. You probably even figured out the order in which the steps needed to be completed. Perhaps you wrote down the steps.

Time to think about your goals.

On the following pages you'll find tips on how to write goals and a place to write down some of your goals. You'll check whether each goal is short-term or long-range, and write in the date by which you plan to accomplish each goal. You'll then write the steps to achieving your goal.

Happy Goal Setting!

Set Your Goals

Why is setting goals so important? Because goals can help you do, be, and experience everything you want in life. Instead of just letting life happen to you, goals help you to create the life you want. When you set goals, you are taking control of your life. Think of it this way: Goals are like having a map that keeps you on the right road, going in the right direction to where you want to be in life.

In the following spaces take a few minutes to write out some of your goals.

GOAL #1 _____

_____

_____ **Short Term** _____ **Long Range**   **Target Date** _____

GOAL #2 _____

_____

_____ **Short Term** _____ **Long Range**   **Target Date** _____

GOAL #3 _____

_____

_____ **Short Term** _____ **Long Range**   **Target Date** _____

Describe roadblocks that might interfere with your reaching each goal.
List strategies for overcoming each roadblock.

	Roadblocks	**Strategies**
Goal #1	_____	_____
	_____	_____
Goal #2	_____	_____
	_____	_____
Goal #3	_____	_____
	_____	_____

Keeping Track of My Goals

Goal #1

Steps Toward Achieving My Goal:

	Review Date	Step Achieved	Step Not Achieved
1. _____			
2. _____			
3. _____			
4. _____			

Goal #2

Steps Toward Achieving My Goal:

	Review Date	Step Achieved	Step Not Achieved
1. _____			
2. _____			
3. _____			
4. _____			

Goal #3

Steps Toward Achieving My Goal:

	Review Date	Step Achieved	Step Not Achieved
1. _____			
2. _____			
3. _____			
4. _____			

What You See Is What You Get

The greatest discovery of my generation is that human beings, by changing the inner attitudes of their minds, can change the outer aspects of their lives.

—William James

What do you think William James meant when he made that statement? James may not have been familiar with the term, but what he was talking about was *visualization*. Visualizing is something everybody does, every day. When you daydream, think about someone you know, or remember a place you visited in the past, you are visualizing. And you can make the technique of visualization *work for you*. You can use it to help achieve your goals. Here's how:

As clearly and realistically as possible, visualize your desired goal as if it were already reality. Hang this picture in your mental gallery, and look at it often. Your visualization will help you stay focused on your goal and able to take advantage of all the opportunities that come along that may help you reach your goal.

Create a Treasure Map

This fun activity will help you develop the ability to visualize your goal. Paint or draw a treasure map—an actual, physical picture of your goal. Make it a clear, sharp image that you can focus on. If you like, instead of (or in addition to) drawing your treasure map, cut out pictures and words from magazines and make a collage. Follow these tips below to create your personal treasure map:

Tips for Creating Your Treasure Map

1. Do a treasure map for a single goal—don't try to include several goals.

2. Put YOU in the picture. Use a photo or draw an image of yourself.

3. Show the complete and glorious outcome of your goal.

4. Use lots of color. Color can have quite an impact on your mind.

5. Make the size of your treasure map work for you—whether you want to carry it in your notebook or hang on your wall.

6. Have **FUN!!!**

What You Say Is What You Get

One of the best tools for triggering positive pictures and feelings within you is an *affirmation*. An affirmation is a strong, positive statement that describes something (your goal, perhaps) as FACT. Affirmations work in the subconscious mind by replacing uncertainty, doubt, and apathy with confidence and conviction.

Affirmations are designed to:

- stimulate your subconscious to be continuously alert to situations that will further your goal.
- signal your conscious mind to actively engage in those situations.

When designing and writing your affirmations, follow the guidelines below:

Affirmations should be:

Under Your Control
Affirmations must be personal and under your control. You cannot affirm or alter situations that you do not control.

Stated in Positive Language
Write affirmations in positive language. You must use vivid words and phrases to describe what you want. For example, don't say "I am no longer unorganized." Instead say, "I am a neat and organized person."

Present Tense
Write affirmations in the present tense. The subconscious mind only operates in the "now." If you create affirmations in the future tense, your subconscious will never get there.

As Though Already Achieved
Write affirmations as if you have already achieved your goal. Don't say "I will." "I have" and "I am" are more powerful. By describing your goal as already achieved, you are clearly conveying the desired outcome to your subconscious.

Convey Action and Emotion
Begin affirmations with words that convey action and emotion. Words like "I easily," and "I quickly" convey action. Words like "I confidently" and "I enthusiastically" show emotion. Action and feeling words make your affirmation more believable and attractive.

Realistic
Affirmations must be realistic. Develop affirmations that aim for excellence not perfection. Write affirmations that have a good chance of happening.

Here are some examples of positive, well written affirmations:

I express myself well, and I know others respect my point of view.

I enthusiastically do my homework every night.

I am happily involved in a variety of interests in my school and community.

I willingly help my family members in any way I can.

I am a good friend and I enjoy my relationships.

Now, think back to the goals you wrote in an earlier activity. Follow the guidelines outlined above, and write two affirmations for each goal.

Goal #1:
Affirmation 1: _____

_____

Affirmation 2:_____

_____

Goal #2:
Affirmation 1: _____

_____

Affirmation 2: _____

_____

Goal #3:
Affirmation 1: _____

_____

Affirmation 2:_____

_____

Now put your affirmations to work.

• Read your affirmation several times each day.

• When you read the affirmations, look at or think of your treasure map at the same time. The words and picture (affirmations and visualization) reinforce each other.

• Really *feel* your affirmation. Enjoy the positive feeling of accomplishment each time you repeat your affirmation.

The degree to which your affirmation impacts your subconscious depends on *how* you use it and *how often* you use it. Compare these percentages.
Reading the affirmation
       = 10% impact
Reading and visualizing
       = 55% impact
Reading, visualizing and *feeling*
       = 100% impact

A Pat on the Back

When you have set and accomplished a goal, congratulate yourself! Reward yourself, too! Think of one nice thing you can do for yourself when you have achieved each of your goals. Describe it here:

Goal #1:

_____

_____

How I will reward myself:

_____

_____

Goal #2:

_____

_____

How I will reward myself:

_____

_____

Goal #3:

_____

_____

How I will reward myself:

_____

_____

_____

Decision Making
&
Problem Solving

You make many decisions every day. Many are quick, easy decisions like what to eat and what to wear. Others are a little more involved, like deciding what subject to write a report on or whether or not to run for student council representative.

Generally speaking, the more important the decision, the more conscious effort you need to put into making it. Good decision making involves using information to make choices. Information like:

—your values and goals
—people and things that influence you
—the various alternatives you have
—the likely consequences of choosing each alternative

Problem solving is similar to decision making. You still need to use information and make choices; however, solving a problem usually involves more than one decision. It's a more complicated process.

The Decision-Making Process

You may not realize it but you are making decisions all the time everyday. Things like what to wear to school or what to do on Friday night with your friends are examples of little decisions you're always making. But in addition to these common, everyday decisions you often have to make big important decision like what will you do after high school – go to college or get a job, which car to buy – the big pickup with low gas mileage or the small fuel efficient car that gets great gas mileage. Learning effective decision-making skills will increase the possibility that you will make a good decision so that you will get what you really want

Here are some steps to follow when you have a decision to make:
1. Recognize and define the decision to be made.
2. Know what is important to you—your values—and what you want to accomplish—your goal.
3. Study the information you already have, and obtain and study new information, too.
4. List all of your alternatives.
5. List the advantages and disadvantages of each alternative.
6. Make a decision.
7. Develop a plan for carrying out your decision.

Now let's see how the process really works.

1. Think of a decision that you need to make in the next month. Define it here:

_____

_____

2. What kinds of things that are important in your life (your values) might affect, or be affected by, this decision?

_____

_____

_____

3. What kinds of information do you have or need?

Things to think about: _____

_____

_____

People to talk to: _____

_____

_____

Things to read: _____

_____

_____

Things to do: _____

_____

_____

4. & 5. What are your alternatives and what are the advantages and disadvantages of each?

ALTERNATIVE 1	
Advantages	**Disadvantages**

ALTERNATIVE 2	
Advantages	**Disadvantages**

ALTERNATIVE 3	
Advantages	**Disadvantages**

Decision Point!

6. Which alternative has the best chance of producing the outcome you want?

More About Decisions...

Write down all the decisions that you can remember making so far today. For example, you probably made decisions about what to wear, what to eat, how to spend your breaks and with whom. You may have made decisions about whether to go to class, how to approach an assignment, what to say to someone, and whether to tell the truth. Include all types of decisions on your list.

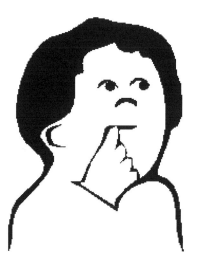

Decisions

1. _____

2. _____

3. _____

4. _____

5. _____

6. _____

7. _____

8. _____

9. _____

Now go back through your list of decisions and code each one with a number from this scale.

0 = I have no control over this type of decision; it is dictated by others.

1 = This type of decision is automatic, routine, or habitual.

2 = I occasionally think about this type of decision.

3 = I think about this type of decision, but I don't study it.

4 = I study this type of decision somewhat.

5 = I study this type of decision a lot.

What does this exercise tell you about how you make most of your decisions?

_____

_____

_____

_____

_____

_____

_____

What is the worst decision you ever made? Write a brief description of it:

_____

_____

_____

_____

_____

_____

_____

Decision or Outcome? Next time you're tempted to kick yourself over a "bad" decision, consider this:

✤ When you say that a decision is poor, you probably mean the *result* or *outcome* is not what you wanted.

✤ Good decision making minimizes the possibility of getting bad outcomes, but it doesn't eliminate the possibility.

✤ A *decision* is the act of choosing among several possibilities based on your judgments.

✤ An *outcome* is the result, consequence, or aftermath of the decision.

✤ You have direct control over the decision, but *not* over the outcome.

✤ A good decision does not guarantee a good outcome, but it does increase the chances of a good outcome.

Go back and look at your "worst" decision again. Was it really a bad decision, or was it a reasonable decision with a bad outcome?

Your Alternatives

Think of a decision you need to make. Describe it here: _____

_____

_____

What are you able to do in this situation? Write down as many realistic alternatives as you can think of.

_____   _____

_____   _____

_____   _____

_____   _____

Go back and circle all of the alternatives you are willing to try.

One of the best ways to increase your chances of making a good decision is to increase your alternatives. Write down as many ideas as you can think of for increasing your alternatives.

1. _____
2. _____
3. _____
4. _____
5. _____
6. _____
7. _____
8. _____
9. _____
10. _____

Remember: In decision making, information is your biggest ally.

The Choices I've Made

Dan starts a class he doesn't enjoy much, and after a couple of days he says to himself, "I'm not interested in anything being covered in this class. I don't have to take it to graduate, so I'm going to transfer to a class that I'll be able to use, one that I'll enjoy." And he does.

Maria has similar feelings about a class. But after thinking it over, she decides that since the class is in her major field of interest, she'll stick with it. As the semester continues, Maria finds that the class gets more interesting.

Suzanne feels the same way about a class she signed up for, but doesn't transfer to another one. She doesn't want to disappoint her parents or cause anyone to think she isn't capable of handling the class.

Dan, Suzanne, and Maria all face a similar situation, but each reacts differently. Suzanne's decision is based on what she imagines other people will think, rather than her own needs. Dan and Maria decide to do different things, but both of them make thoughtful decisions based on their own needs and values.

Think of a decision you made recently that worked out well.

What was it? Who and/or what influenced your decision?
    __Your needs (things you can't get along without)
    __Your values (what you like)
    __Your goals (what you want to accomplish)
    __Other people... Who?

_____

_____

    __Advertising
    __Other...What?

_____

_____

Sometimes making decisions can be frustrating.

For weeks, Ryan has been working on his car. He has spent all his money and every available hour getting it fixed up for a custom car show. Now, the day before the show, some of his friends invite him to go with them to the river tomorrow. Ryan really enjoys going to the river, but he wants to enter his car in the show, too. Both things are happening on the same day. It makes him mad that he has to choose between two things he wants.

Has anything like this ever happened to you? How did you feel at the time?

What did you do?

Sometimes we decide not to decide.

The coach asks Tom if he wants to be on the track team, which makes Tom feel great, except that he is nervous about being the newest and least experienced person on the team. So Tom puts off making a decision. Accidentally (on purpose) he forgets to let the coach know by the deadline. A day or two later Tom says to himself, "Too bad I forgot about notifying Coach that I wanted to be on the track team. Oh, well."

Have you ever put off making a decision? If you could get that day back, what would you do this time?

Sometimes decisions are risky.

Sheila thinks she wants to go to college, but she isn't sure what it will be like. She's been planning to go to a nearby community college for two years while continuing to live at home. Then she finds out that she could live with her aunt in the city and go to a well-known four-year college. Sheila doesn't know if she really wants to leave home yet, if she wants to live with her aunt, or which college will be the better choice.

What do you think Sheila should do?

___ Live at home and go to the community college.

___ Live with her aunt and go to the four-year college.

___ Get a lot more information before making a decision.

What types of information does Sheila need? **List at least four categories here:**

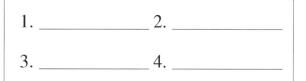

1. _____   2. _____

3. _____   4. _____

Try this:

Next time you watch a movie or TV show, notice the decisions the characters in the story make. You will probably think some of the decisions are reasonable and others will seem wrong or foolish. See if you can analyze how each decision was made.

Steps for Solving a Problem Responsibly

What is a problem?

A problem can be a complicated issue or question that you have to answer. Or it can be something in your life that is causing you frustration, worry, anger, or some other kind of distress. In order to answer the question or get rid of the distress, you must "solve" the problem. Problems often have several parts. Solving the whole problem involves making a series of decisions — at least one decision for each part of the problem.

Next time you are faced with a problem, follow these steps to a solution:

1. Stop all blaming.

It will help me to understand that blaming someone (including myself) for the problem will not solve it. If I really want to solve the problem, I need to put my energy into working out a solution. Blaming myself and others is a waste of time.

2. Define the problem.

Next, I need to ask myself two questions to help me get started. "What exactly is the problem?" and "Whose problem is it?" If I find that it's not my problem, the best thing I can do is let the people who "own" the problem solve it themselves. Or I can ask them, "How can I help you?"

3. Consider asking for help.

Once I'm sure I "own" the problem and know what it is, I may choose to ask someone for help. For example, I may decide to talk over the problem with someone I trust.

4. Think of alternative solutions.

I need to ask myself, "What are some things I could do about this?" I need to think of as many reasonable ideas for solving the problem as I can. To do this, I will probably need to collect some information.

5. Evaluate the alternatives.

Next, for each idea I come up with, I need to ask myself, "What will happen to me and the other people involved if I try this one?" I need to be very honest with myself. If I don't know how someone else will be affected, I need to ask that person, "How will you feel about it if I..."

6. Make a decision.

I need to choose the alternative that appears to have the best chance of succeeding. If my solution is a responsible one, it will not hurt anyone unnecessarily—and it will probably work.

7. Follow through.

After I've made the decision, I'll stick to it for a reasonable length of time. If the decision doesn't work, I'll try another alternative. If the decision works, but causes more problems in the process, I'll start all over again to solve them. And I'll try not to blame myself or anybody else for those problems.

The Problem-Solving Process

Now take a look at a problem you're having and go through the problem-solving process to try to resolve it.

1. Stop Blaming

Have you blamed someone or something else, or yourself for this problem? Blaming doesn't help, and it won't solve the problem. Say to yourself, "This is my problem, and I will do my best to solve it."

2. Define the problem

First, ask if this is really your problem. If it is someone else's problem, the best thing you can do is let them solve it. If it's your problem, in order to get a handle on it, you need to describe your problem in as much detail as possible

Briefly identify your problem: _____

_____

Now, elaborate on the problem in more detail: _____

_____

_____

_____

_____

_____

_____

_____

_____

_____

_____

3. Do I need help?

People who care about you are usually happy to offer assistance when you ask them for help. But don't try to get them to solve the problem for you. That job is up to you. Ask the other person to listen and make suggestions.

Make a list of all the people you can ask for help:

_____   _____

_____   _____

_____   _____

_____   _____

_____   _____

_____   _____

4. How many alternative solutions can I think of?

Ask yourself, "What are some things I can do to solve my problem?" It's a good idea to write down all the ideas you came up with and those that are suggested by others. That way you won't forget any of them.

Write your alternatives here:

1. _____

   _____

2. _____

   _____

3. _____

   _____

(If you have more alternatives, use another sheet of paper.)

5. Consider the consequences of each alternative

This can take some time and plenty of thought to really think through the impact of each alternative. Carefully think over each alternative solution you came up with in step 4, and ask yourself, "What will happen to me and the other people involved if I try this idea?"

Write down the consequences of each alternative solution here:

1. _____

_____

_____

_____

_____

_____

2. _____

_____

_____

_____

_____

_____

3. _____

_____

_____

_____

_____

_____

6. Decision time

Go ahead and make a decision. If you have done all the steps before this one, your decision will probably be a good one.

Describe what you are going to do to solve the problem:

_____

_____

_____

_____

_____

_____

_____

_____

_____

_____

7. Stick to the decision

Once you decide what to do and carry out your decision, give your decision a chance to work. Remember, if it doesn't work, or causes more problems, don't blame yourself. You did the best you could. **Just start over again with the steps for solving the problem and select another alternative solution to give a try.**

Remember, this is a process you can use throughout your life in any circumstance where you're facing a problem. You never have to feel helpless against problems that come up.

Team Building

Six students who sit at different desks, work on individual assignments, and receive separate grades are not a team. However, when they pull their desks close or sit around a table and work on a project together, they start to become a team.

If you've ever been on a softball team, football team, soccer team, debate team, cheer leading team, or any other kind of team, you know that "teamwork" doesn't just happen. It takes time, effort, and practice for a group of people to function like a true team.

To be successful now and in the future, you'll have to work with many different teams of people, so one of the most important skills you can learn is how to help groups function smoothly—so that every person is respected, the skills and talents of each member are utilized, problems are solved cooperatively, and everyone works toward the same goal.

How to Become a Team

Teams are never created instantly. They have to evolve. As a group works together, it goes through certain stages of development—much like a child goes through different stages as he or she grows up.

STAGES OF GROUP DEVELOPMENT

STAGE 1:

The team looks for leadership and directions.

Members look at each other and ask, "What are we supposed to do?" They feel somewhat confused. Maybe they ask their teacher or boss for help. At some point, however, they realize that if they're going to be a team, they have to start acting like one.

STAGE 2:

The team starts to organize. Conflicts emerge and are settled.

How do members act like a team? Well first, they have to figure out all the different parts of the job. They have to answer the "who," "what," "when," "where," and "how" questions that are part of getting organized. In the process, members sometimes disagree about who should do things and how they should be done.

STAGE 3:

Information flows freely and members feel good about the team.

By the time it reaches this stage, the team is organized and conflicts have been settled. Members find themselves working together extremely well. They still disagree sometimes, but now conflicts are seen as natural and members have found effective ways to resolve them.

STAGE 4:

The team can solve problems. Members are interdependent.

At this stage, the team seems to be able to tackle anything. Creative ideas are abundant. Members work alone, in pairs, or as a total group with equal success. Every member of the team is valued and is depended upon by every other member.

Think of a group or team to which you have belonged. It can be an athletic team, a club, or a group of friends. Reread the "Stages of Group Development" while remembering your group or team. Then carefully answer these questions:

1. Name of the group:

_____

2. Purpose/goal of the group:

_____

_____

_____

_____

3. What stage of development did the group reach?

_____

_____

4. What specific incidents and/or group behaviors support your conclusion? Describe at least three here:

1. _____

_____

_____

2. _____

_____

3. _____

_____

The Team and Me

Take this Self-Assessment to help you think about your behavior in a recent group or team situation. Read through the list and put a check in the appropriate column after each behavior.

	About right	Need to do more of	Need to do less of
Communication Skills			
1. contributing to group discussions			
2. listening actively			
3. inviting others to speak			
4. staying on the topic			
Leadership Skills			
5. sharing a vision of the future			
6. giving directions and information			
7. inspiring/encouraging others			
8. pitching in and helping others			
Problem-Solving Skills			
9. stating problems and goals			
10. asking for ideas and opinions			
11. offering your own ideas			
12. evaluating ideas			

	About right	Need to do more of	Need to do less of
Team-Building Skills			
13. demonstrating commitment to group			
14. expressing appreciation of others			
15. helping achieve consensus/agreement			
16. helping to reduce tension			
17. helping to resolve conflicts			
Expressing Feelings			
18. telling others what I feel			
19. disagreeing openly			
20. being sarcastic or putting others down			
21. expressing humor			
Getting Along with Others			
22. competing to outdo others			
23. dominating the group			
24. including others			
25. criticizing others			
26. helping others			
27. being patient			

Look at how you rated yourself. Do you feel that you need to improve any of your group skills or behaviors? Develop a goal in one area and write it here:

My goal is to... _____

_____

_____

Leadership

Sometimes you are a leader. Sometimes you are a follower. Depending on the situation, everyone plays both roles — and that includes you.

When you show a classmate how to solve an algebra problem, when you persuade your friends to go to a particular movie, or when you give directions to a visitor who is lost, you are being a leader. When you ask for directions, let someone else choose the movie, or request help with a geometry problem, you are being a follower.

As you will see, there are many ways to be a leader. The more ways — or styles — you learn and practice, the more opportunities you will have to lead.

Interview a Leader

Interview someone who is a leader. You might decide to interview a person who supervises others as part of his or her job, or the leader of a community organization, like the YMCA, an environmental group, a service club, or a neighborhood co-op. The person might even be a political leader, like a council member, mayor, or school board member. Use these questions and develop two of your own.

1. What is your title or position?

_____

2. What are your main responsibilities in the position?

_____

_____

3. How much of your job involves leadership?

_____

4. To whom do you provide leadership?

_____

5. Specifically what do you do as a leader?

_____

_____

_____

6. What personal qualities do you think are required to be a successful leader?

_____

_____

7. What suggestions do you have for young people who want to become leaders?

_____

_____

_____

8. (Your question) _____

_____

_____

9. (Your question) _____

_____

_____

Identifying Leadership Styles

Read through the different leadership styles below, and put a ✔ beside the style of leadership being provided in each situation.

Cindy and Tom are two students at a very large public high school. Both have disabilities. Cindy has cystic fibrosis and Tom has a spinal-cord injury and uses a wheelchair. Cindy and Tom have decided to put their energies into building a more integrated school, one in which students with disabilities are fully included at all levels. They deliver a compelling presentation to the student council, stirring the interest and support of its members.

Cindy and Tom are providing leadership by:

___ giving directions or information.

___ giving encouragement, support, or praise.

___ pitching in, participating, or facilitating.

___ delegating (turning a job over to someone who can do it well).

___ providing vision or inspiration.

providing vision or inspiration.

The student council decides to sponsor an in-school campaign to promote the concept of a fully integrated school in which all students are included, academically and in student government and activities. Brian, the student body president, appoints Leon and Jackie, both art students, to develop some ideas for a logo and posters. He asks Josh to approach the school newspaper about the idea of doing a series of articles. And he appoints Robin and Sheila to work with Tom and Cindy on an overall plan, including some special "events."

Brian is providing leadership by...

___ giving directions or information.

___ giving encouragement, support, or praise.

___ pitching in, participating, or facilitating.

___ delegating (turning a job over to someone who can do it well).

___ providing vision, creativity, or inspiration.

delegating (turning a job over to someone who can do it well).

The school newspaper decides to put out a special edition devoted to the integration theme. Maria, Chris, and Jim are writing the stories. They want to use correct terms and inoffensive language when writing about people with disabilities, but don't have any experience in that area. Ms. Jones, their teacher, gives them a printed summary of the Americans with Disabilities Act, and arranges for Cindy and Tom to come in and advise the entire newspaper staff concerning language and other things they should know.

Ms. Jones, Cindy, and Tom are providing leadership by

___ giving directions or information.
___ giving encouragement, support, or praise.
___ pitching in, participating, or facilitating.
___ delegating (turning a job over to someone who can do it well).
___ providing vision or inspiration.

giving directions or information.

Robin and Sheila are getting ready to videotape a public service announcement for the campaign. The room and the lights are ready, the actors are there, and the camera operator is waiting for directions, but Robin and Sheila are having a disagreement about which of two scripts to use. They don't have time to rehearse and tape both, and there are real differences between the two. Time is wasting. Tony, one of the actors, starts asking questions that get Robin and Sheila to clarify the pros and cons of each script. Before long, they come to an agreement.

Tony is providing leadership by:

___ giving directions or information.
___ giving encouragement, support, or praise.
___ pitching in, participating, or facilitating.
___ delegating (turning a job over to someone who can do it well).
___ providing vision or inspiration.

pitching in, participating, or facilitating.

Carlos decides to run for junior class president. He has the backing of many students, and they help him put together a well-organized campaign. The student council decides to sponsor a panel discussion among all the candidates for class office. Carlos, who has a speech impairment, uses graphic symbols and gestures to help him communicate. He's very reluctant to be on the panel, because he thinks none of the students in the audience will understand him. Richard, the moderator, tells him, "Carlos, we need you. If you can make *me* understand, you can make *anyone* understand. This is no time to back off!" Richard checks with Carlos daily, answering his questions and concerns, right up to the morning of the event.

Richard is providing leadership by:

___ giving directions or information.
___ giving encouragement, support, or praise.
___ pitching in, participating, or facilitating.
___ delegating (turning a job over to someone who can do it well).
___ providing vision or inspiration.

giving encouragement, support, or praise.

What's Your Leadership Style?

What's *your* style? Write about some of your leadership experiences below. Remember, someone takes the lead almost every time two or more people get together.

Think of a time when you were aware that a person or group was in the dark about what to do. So you gave them directions or information. Maybe you walked them step-by-step through the task. Write about it here:

_____

_____

_____

Now write about a time when someone was discouraged or insecure about his or her ability to accomplish something. You knew the person could do it, so you offered him or her lots of encouragement and praise—and it worked!

_____

_____

_____

_____

Describe a time when you observed that a project or activity was bogged down, so you jumped in and helped out, and got it going again.

_____

_____

_____

_____

Describe a time when you recognized that something needed to be done, so you found someone who could handle the job, and asked that person to take over.

_____

_____

_____

Write about a time when you had an idea or vision of something that you wanted to have happen. By sharing your vision with some other people, you motivated them to help. Eventually, your dream became reality.

_____

_____

_____

Leadership and You

Leadership is a process, not a person. Everyone needs leadership some times, and everyone gives leadership at other times. What exactly is leadership?

Leadership is the process of influencing another person or a group of people to move in the direction of a goal.

Depending on the situation, a leader may:
- give directions and information.
- give encouragement and praise.
- get involved—help solve a problem, lead a discussion, etc.
- delegate a job to someone who is qualified to do it.
- provide vision and inspire others to do their best.

Think of a time when you were a leader. Describe the situation here:

_____

_____

What kind(s) of leadership did you provide?

_____

_____

What kinds of leadership do *you* need at school? Consider each one of your classes. List the subject and then put a ✔ next to the number that best describes how you feel about that class:

Subject: _____

____ **1.** I don't understand the subject at all. I don't even like to go to class.
____ **2.** I have some trouble with the subject, but it's interesting and I enjoy the class.
____ **3.** I can get good grades in the subject, but it really doesn't interest me.
____ **4.** I do very well in the subject and I enjoy it, too.

Subject: _____

____ **1.** I don't understand the subject at all. I don't even like to go to class.
____ **2.** I have some trouble with the subject, but it's interesting and I enjoy the class.
____ **3.** I can get good grades in the subject, but it really doesn't interest me.
____ **4.** I do very well in the subject and I enjoy it, too.

Subject: _____

___ **1.** I don't understand the subject at all. I don't even like to go to class.
___ **2.** I have some trouble with the subject, but it's interesting and I enjoy the class.
___ **3.** I can get good grades in the subject, but it really doesn't interest me.
___ **4.** I do very well in the subject and I enjoy it, too.

Subject: _____

___ **1.** I don't understand the subject at all. I don't even like to go to class.
___ **2.** I have some trouble with the subject, but it's interesting and I enjoy the class.
___ **3.** I can get good grades in the subject, but it really doesn't interest me.
___ **4.** I do very well in the subject and I enjoy it, too.

Subject: _____

___ **1.** I don't understand the subject at all. I don't even like to go to class.
___ **2.** I have some trouble with the subject, but it's interesting and I enjoy the class.
___ **3.** I can get good grades in the subject, but it really doesn't interest me.
___ **4.** I do very well in the subject and I enjoy it, too.

Subject: _____

___ **1.** I don't understand the subject at all. I don't even like to go to class.
___ **2.** I have some trouble with the subject, but it's interesting and I enjoy the class.
___ **3.** I can get good grades in the subject, but it really doesn't interest me.
___ **4.** I do very well in the subject and I enjoy it, too.

Subject: _____

___ **1.** I don't understand the subject at all. I don't even like to go to class.
___ **2.** I have some trouble with the subject, but I it's interesting and I enjoy the class.
___ **3.** I can get good grades in the subject, but it really doesn't interest me.
___ **4.** I do very well in the subject and I enjoy it, too.

Look on the next page to find out what kind of leadership you need from the teacher in each of your classes.

For each number you checked, read the corresponding paragraph to find out what kind of leadership you need.

1. You need lots of help and supervision. Ask your teacher, a parent, a tutor, or another student for step-by-step directions on each assignment. Have your work checked frequently. You benefit most from a teacher who is a "**director**." One who lets you know exactly what is expected of you and coaches you through each assignment. You do not have to feel lost and confused. Don't accept these feelings. Ask for the help you need. Don't worry about liking the class. As soon as you know what you're doing, you'll begin to enjoy it.

2. You need direction and supervision as you continue to gain skill in the class. Whenever you don't understand a problem or assignment, ask for clarification. You benefit most from a teacher who is a "**motivator**." One who sees that you're catching on, gives you lots of positive reinforcement, and inspires you to try even harder. The other thing that will help you is to get involved in the class. You know enough to ask lots of questions and contribute to discussions. Do it. This will reinforce your enjoyment of the class and help you pick up the missing skills faster.

3. You are bored with either the subject or the class or both. If you don't need the class, consider substituting one that you like. If the class is required, take responsibility for increasing your levels of participation and enjoyment. Volunteer for an extra-credit assignment that challenges you. Get involved in class discussions. Volunteer for group assignments. You benefit most from a teacher who is a "**participator**." One who invites lots of class participation, interaction, and collaboration. If that's not your teacher's style, see if you can transfer to another teacher.

4. You are so successful and self-motivated in this class that you don't need much leadership at all. You will do the work whether the teacher is there or not. You benefit most from a teacher who is a "**delegator**." One who trusts you enough to say, "Here's the assignment—see what you can do with it." This class offers *you* a chance to be a leader. Be creative. Break new ground. Offer to help students who are having trouble with the class. If you see ways that the class could be improved for everyone, discuss them privately with the teacher.

The teacher is your leader. Ask for the help you need!

Conflict Resolution

There are times when individuals or groups disagree. They have different ideas about what should be done and how to do it. They may debate an issue, argue about a decision, or bicker over some little detail.

Conflict is normal, and so are the angry feelings that sometimes go with it. Conflict usually means that people have different ideas, and that's actually good. The more ideas an individual or a group can come up with, the more choices it has. The trick is to know how to manage conflict, use it to produce good results, and resolve it peacefully. This section will show you how.

Conflict Observation Sheet

Directions: Observe one different conflict every day for the next six days. It can be a real conflict between adults, teens, or children, or a dramatized conflict on TV or in a movie. Don't get involved. Just watch. As soon as you can after the conflict has ended, write down your answers to the following questions.

Day 1

What was the conflict about?

_____

_____

How many people were involved? _____

Describe what happened:

_____

_____

_____

_____

Check all methods that were used to resolve or end the conflict:
___ fight or argument
___ listening to each other
___ apologizing
___ sharing or taking turns
___ humor
___ compromise
___ asking for help
___ problem solving or negotiation
___ other (describe below)

_____

_____

What ideas do you have for resolving the conflict?

_____

_____

_____

Day 2

What was the conflict about?

_____

_____

How many people were involved? _____

Describe what happened:

_____

_____

_____

_____

Check all methods that were used to resolve or end the conflict:
___ fight or argument
___ listening to each other
___ apologizing
___ sharing or taking turns
___ humor
___ compromise
___ asking for help
___ problem solving or negotiation
___ other (describe below)

_____

_____

What ideas do you have for resolving the conflict?

_____

_____

_____

Day 3

What was the conflict about?

_____

_____

_____

_____

How many people were involved? _____

Describe what happened:

_____

_____

_____

_____

Check all methods that were used to resolve or end the conflict:
___ fight or argument
___ listening to each other
___ apologizing
___ sharing or taking turns
___ humor
___ compromise
___ asking for help
___ problem solving or negotiation
___ other (describe below)

_____

_____

_____

What ideas do you have for resolving the conflict?

_____

_____

_____

Day 4

What was the conflict about?

_____

_____

_____

_____

How many people were involved? _____

Describe what happened:

_____

_____

_____

_____

Check all methods that were used to resolve or end the conflict:
___ fight or argument
___ listening to each other
___ apologizing
___ sharing or taking turns
___ humor
___ compromise
___ asking for help
___ problem solving or negotiation
___ other (describe below)

_____

_____

_____

What ideas do you have for resolving the conflict?

_____

_____

_____

Day 5

What was the conflict about?

_____

_____

_____

_____

How many people were involved? _____

Describe what happened:

_____

_____

_____

Check all methods that were used to resolve or end the conflict:

____ fight or argument
____ listening to each other
____ apologizing
____ sharing or taking turns
____ humor
____ compromise
____ asking for help
____ problem solving or negotiation
____ other (describe below)

_____

_____

_____

_____

What ideas do you have for resolving the conflict?

_____

_____

_____

Day 6

What was the conflict about?

_____

_____

_____

_____

How many people were involved? _____

Describe what happened:

_____

_____

_____

Check all methods that were used to resolve or end the conflict:

____ fight or argument
____ listening to each other
____ apologizing
____ sharing or taking turns
____ humor
____ compromise
____ asking for help
____ problem solving or negotiation
____ other (describe below)

_____

_____

_____

_____

What ideas do you have for resolving the conflict?

_____

_____

_____

Real Ways to Resolve a Conflict

Here are 9 different conflict resolution strategies with which you need to become familiar. Depending on the type of conflict you are involved in, try out one (or more) of these strategies and see what happens

1. Listen carefully to the other person.

Let the other person explain his or her side of the story. Pay close attention and try to understand the person's point of view.

2. Explain your position without blaming the other person.

Tell your side of the story and express your feelings in a non-threatening way. Use I-statements such as "I feel angry" or "I'm upset" instead of saying, "You made me mad." Using I-statements makes it easier for the other person to listen to you.

3. Allow time to cool off.

If either of you is extremely angry, tired, or "out-of-control, " it may be better to agree on a later time to deal with the problem. Allowing a cooling off time for one or both of you may prevent a bigger conflict.

4. Problem solve together to create a "win-win" situation.

Make it your goal to find a resolution that both of you can accept. This is best done when both of you are calm enough to consider the other's point of view. You may need to try one or more other strategies first, such as apologizing or listening carefully to the other person's side of the story. Problem solving may also lead to compromise.

5. Be willing to compromise.

Both persons in a conflict must cooperate in order to reach a compromise. You will probably have to give up something, but you will get something, too. Use problem solving to reach a compromise both of you can agree on.

6. Use humor.

Making light of a conflict, without making fun of the other person, may ease the tension both of you feel. Humor generally works best when you direct it toward yourself in a natural, lighthearted way. This may help the other person realize that the situation isn't as bad as it seems.

7. Say you're sorry.

If you're responsible for the conflict, say, "I'm sorry, I didn't mean to do it," or "I'm sorry we got into this fight." Saying, "I'm sorry," doesn't necessarily mean that you are admitting any wrongdoing. "I'm sorry" can just be a way of saying, "I know you are hurt and angry and I feel bad about that." A problem often gets worse when one person feels badly and thinks the other person doesn't care — or care enough. This feeling can be eased by a simple "I'm sorry."

8. Ask for help.

When no one can suggest a solution, it's best to ask someone else to step in and help resolve the conflict. The new person can bring new ideas and a fresh perspective to the problem.

9. Know when to walk away.

If you find yourself in a situation where you might be physically hurt, walk or run away. If you think the other person might become violent, it's best to say you're sorry and leave quickly rather than try to save face or be tough.

Managing Conflict By Controlling Anger

Anger is an emotion that everyone feels at times. Like conflict, it's a normal part of life. Anger isn't bad or good, it's just a feeling, but it can lead to bad outcomes if it's not managed appropriately. Volatile expressions of anger can lead to conflict, negatively affect relationships and have negative health consequences as well.

There are healthy and appropriate ways to manage anger. The important thing to remember is that it's not the situation that makes us angry, it's how we react to a situation that causes us to be angry. If you know what makes you angry, you can learn to recognize the onset of angry feelings and can do something to calm down and cool down. A cool, calm body will always help you to manage your anger and conflicts better.

Answer the following questions to get more in touch with how you handle anger.

What generally makes you angry? _____

_____

_____

Have you felt angry in the past week? _____

What provoked your anger? _____

_____

_____

What happens when you are unable to control your anger?

_____

_____

What happens if you let anger build up for hours or days?

_____

_____

What have you done in the past to control anger? _____

_____

_____

What new ideas for controlling anger can you try? _____

_____

_____

_____

Why is it important to learn strategies to control anger? _____

_____

_____

_____

Write about a time you managed anger well. _____

_____

_____

_____

_____

_____

_____

In the future when you find yourself in a situation that normally makes you angry
what can you do to manage your anger so it doesn't get the best of you?

_____

_____

_____

_____

_____

_____

_____

Self-Determination & Personal Mastery

Who determines who you are and what you become? You do. Who is in charge of your future? You are. Who must stand up for your needs? You must.

Sure, other people care about you. And because you are not yet an adult, other people often tell you what to do, where to go, and how to behave. Nevertheless, the person with the most control over your life, now and for as long as you live, is you.

The exercises on the next few pages will help you recognize your true capabilities and ways in which you limit yourself. You will also practice being assertive in standing up for your rights and resisting pressure from your peers and others.

The Jar of Fleas

Overcoming Challenges and Limitations

Read this story, and then answer the questions the following pages

Old Harry Fretchit wanted to train some new fleas for his flea circus, so he hung out with some cats and dogs until he caught about ten nice, strong, high-jumping fleas. Harry wanted fleas that were strong and healthy, so the higher they jumped, the better. But you can't train a flea who can jump clear across the room without first getting its attention.

So high jumping was the first habit of Harry's new fleas that he had to break. How he did it was very interesting.

At first, the fleas were in a big cage where they had plenty of jumping room. So Harry patiently transferred them to a jar about five inches high. After that, each time a flea jumped, he banged his whole body on the lid of the jar. Obviously, continual body banging felt very uncomfortable to the fleas. As a result, they began to jump with less vigor, so that when they banged

themselves it wouldn't hurt so bad (but it still hurt). After a while, they jumped with even *less* vigor, until finally one flea made a very weak jump and went down again without banging himself at all! As soon as the other fleas saw this, they copied him, and pretty soon all of the fleas were jumping up and down inside the jar without hitting the lid.

Harry had been watching, but he didn't take the lid off—yet. He wanted the fleas to get so used to having the lid there, and jumping little jumps, that they wouldn't miss the lid after it was gone. They would not even *remember* how to make big jumps.

And that's exactly what happened. After several more days, Harry took off the lid and, sure enough, there were those poor little fleas jumping up and down, but never higher than four-and-three-quarters inches for the rest of their lives.

Take a look. Are there any imaginary lids above you?

Write down some of the ways you limit yourself.

1. _____

_____

2. _____

_____

3. _____

_____

Just in case, like the fleas, you've forgotten some of *your* capabilities, take the time to remember them now. Complete the following sentences:

I did something during the first five years of my life that was successful. It was:

_____

_____

During the time I was in elementary school, I succeeded at:

_____

_____

When I was in middle school/junior high school, one of my successes was:

_____

_____

Since I've been in high school, I've succeeded at:

_____

_____

Something I can show other people how to do is:

_____

_____

I am admired by someone for my ability to:

_____

_____

A game I usually win is:

_____

_____

The subject I'm best at in school is:

_____

_____

I feel very proud of myself when I

_____

_____

A job or duty I'm good at is:

_____

_____

A positive habit I've got that I'm pleased with is:

_____

_____

Some people limit themselves because they fear criticism. Other people fear failure. Quite a few fear both. If you fit any of these categories, try to remember to:

1. See and believe in each one of your achievements.

2. Exercise your right to accept or reject criticism based on its worth and value to you.

3. Accept failure as an occasional price of trying.

Five things I like about myself are:

1. _____

_____

2. _____

_____

3. _____

_____

4. _____

_____

5. _____

_____

Acting Assertively

What does it mean to be aggressive, passive, or assertive?

People are aggressive when they:

- intentionally attack, take advantage of, humiliate, hurt, or put down others.
- act on the belief that others are not as important as they are.

The aggressive person's mottos are:

"Get them before they get you."

"How you play doesn't count, only that you win."

"Never give a sucker an even break."

People are passive when they:

- invite, encourage, or permit others to take advantage of them.
- discount themselves and act as if others are more important than they are.

The passive person's mottos are:

"I should never make anyone feel uncomfortable, resentful, or displeased, except myself."

"I should never give anyone a headache or stomachache, except myself."

"I should never disappoint anyone or cause anyone to disapprove of me."

People are assertive when they:

- express themselves openly and honestly to communicate their needs, wants, or feelings, without demanding or discounting the wants, needs, or feelings of others.
- act according to the belief that all people including themselves are equally important.

The assertive person's mottos are:

"I have the right to ask for anything I want."

"If I want something and don't ask for it, I forfeit my right to complain."

"Others have an equal right to ask for what they want."

"I recognize their rights without discounting my own."

Read through the following interactions, and after each of the responses, indicate with a ✔ whether it was passive, aggressive, or assertive.

• Ms. Reynolds, John's history teacher, tells John that his homework is unacceptable, and he must redo it to get a grade. John replies:

1. "I'm so stupid. I never get anything right."

___ passive, ___ aggressive, ___ assertive

2. "No way! That's totally unfair!"

___ passive, ___ aggressive, ___ assertive

3. "I'll do the homework over, Ms. Reynolds, but I need to talk to you first, so that I'll get it right this time."

___ passive, ___ aggressive, ___ assertive

• Tony asks Linda to go to the dance with him. Ross gets mad when he finds out, because he asked Linda, too. Ross tells Tony to back off. Tony replies:

1. "Tough! She wouldn't go with a jerk like you, anyway!"

___ passive, ___ aggressive, ___ assertive

2. "Sure, Ross. Gosh, I'm awful sorry, really."

___ passive, ___ aggressive, ___ assertive

3. "I think I have the right to ask Linda if I want to."

___ passive, ___ aggressive, ___ assertive

• Mary approaches her teacher about a low grade on a written report. She says that because of all her other activities she ran out of time. The teacher says:

1. "You only get what you earn. If you want a better grade, get your priorities straight."

___ passive, ___ aggressive, ___ assertive

2. "Oh, dear! It's my fault for not realizing how busy everyone is."

___ passive, ___ aggressive, ___ assertive

3. "Well, that's too bad."

___ passive, ___ aggressive, ___ assertive

• Lydia asks her friend Alice to help her carry some things to the auditorium. Alice responds:

1. "I'm afraid I'll be late for English, but if you want me to, okay."

___ passive, ___ aggressive, ___ assertive

2. "What's the matter with you? Are your arms broken?"

___ passive, ___ aggressive, ___ assertive

3. "I can't help you right now, Lydia. I have to get to my English class."

___ passive, ___ aggressive, ___ assertive

Passive Aggressive or Assertive

• Aandy returns a pair of jeans to the store because the zipper is broken. The clerk says:

1. "Yes, that's a broken zipper all right. Can I get you another pair?"
___ passive, ___ aggressive, ___ assertive

2. "Oh, I'm so sorry. I should have checked the jeans before I sold them to you. It's all my fault."
___ passive, ___ aggressive, ___ assertive

3. "You broke this zipper didn't you? Well, you're not going to cheat us!"
___ passive, ___ aggressive, ___ assertive

• When she comes home from work, Dan's mother brings his bike in out of the rain. When Dan thanks her, she says:

1. "Oh, don't thank me. I'm gone so much of the time, I should thank you for even being here."
___ passive, ___ aggressive, ___ assertive

2. "If you weren't such a moron, you wouldn't have left it out in the rain in the first place."
___ passive, ___ aggressive, ___ assertive

3. "I'm glad I could help you."
___ passive, ___ aggressive, ___ assertive

• Barbara drives into the parking lot of a small mall, but all the handicapped spaces are taken, so she has to park in a regular spot and then struggle to remove her chair from the back seat. As she's passing one of the handicapped spaces, Barbara almost collides with a young man running to his car. She says:

1. "Thanks to you, Mister, I just had to struggle for 20 minutes getting out of my car. Maybe when you have to pay a fine, you'll stop being so selfish."
___ passive, ___ aggressive, ___ assertive

2. "Hi. I guess maybe you didn't notice that's a handicapped spot?"
___ passive, ___ aggressive, ___ assertive

3. "You violate my rights when you take a spot that's reserved for people with disabilities. I hope you won't do it again."
___ passive, ___ aggressive, ___ assertive

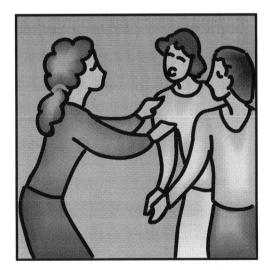

• David's parents have outlined some chores for him to do around the house and yard, but he's fallen behind. His dad threatens to ground David if he doesn't meet his responsibilities before the weekend. David says:

1. "I guess I'm just a worthless slob."
___ passive, ___ aggressive, ___ assertive

2. "You're trying to make my life miserable. This is abuse. You'll be sorry!"
___ passive, ___ aggressive, ___ assertive

3. "I've been concerned about the chores, too. I'll rearrange my schedule and get them done."
___ passive, ___ aggressive, ___ assertive

• Chris realizes, upon leaving the supermarket, that she has been shortchanged 65 cents. She returns, but the cashier denies the mistake. Chris says:

1. "You're a liar. Give me my 65 cents right now!"
___ passive, ___ aggressive, ___ assertive

2. "Well, um, I guess I must have miscounted. Sorry to bother you."
___ passive, ___ aggressive, ___ assertive

3. "I'm sure about this. Here, count the change yourself."
___ passive, ___ aggressive, ___ assertive

As you've been reading and writing, you've probably thought of situations in which you reacted agressively, passively, or assertively. In the space below briefly describe a recent situation in which you behaved either passively or aggressively. Then ask yourself if you could have been more assertive. Describe how you could have behaved more assertively.

Passive or Aggressive behavior: _____

_____

_____

_____

_____

How I could have been Assertive: _____

_____

_____

_____

_____

_____

How Important Is It To Be Included

Is it worth it to be in? What have you done to be included in a group?

YES or NO   **I have...**

____ ____ risked losing friends.

____ ____ hurt people who thought they were my friends by making them feel left out.

____ ____ done something I thought was not right.

____ ____ done something I knew was against the law.

____ ____ drunk alcohol or used drugs.

____ ____ done something that might have harmed my physically.

____ ____ done something that cost me a lot of money.

____ ____ done something that interfered with my school work.

____ ____ done something my parents would have objected to if they had known.

____ ____ done whatever was necessary, as long as it didn't harm anyone else.

____ ____ done something that was against my religion.

____ ____ done whatever was necessary.

Can you remember a time when you were pressured to exclude someone from an activity? _____

How did you feel? _____

_____

What did you do? _____

_____

_____

If this ever happens again, what do you think you will do? _____

_____

_____

Responding to Peer Pressure

It's normal to want to fit in and feel accepted and liked. Sometimes this need is so strong, we are tempted to do almost anything to satisfy it — including things we shouldn't do. When other teens try to get you to do something that is wrong or dangerous, it's called *peer pressure*.

Think of a peer-pressure situation that is happening in your life right now. Or think of one that has happened recently.

Write a brief description of the situation here:

_____

_____

_____

_____

_____

Now answer these questions:

1. What are your peers asking you to do?

_____

_____

_____

_____

2. Do you really want to do it?

_____

3. What are the consequences of doing it? What might happen to you and other people if you do it?

_____

_____

_____

_____

_____

_____

4. Does doing this fit with your beliefs, values, and/or goals? How?

_____

_____

_____

5. Is doing this really good for you? How will you benefit?

_____

_____

_____

_____

_____

6. If not, what other choices do you have?

_____

_____

_____

_____

_____

_____

_____

_____

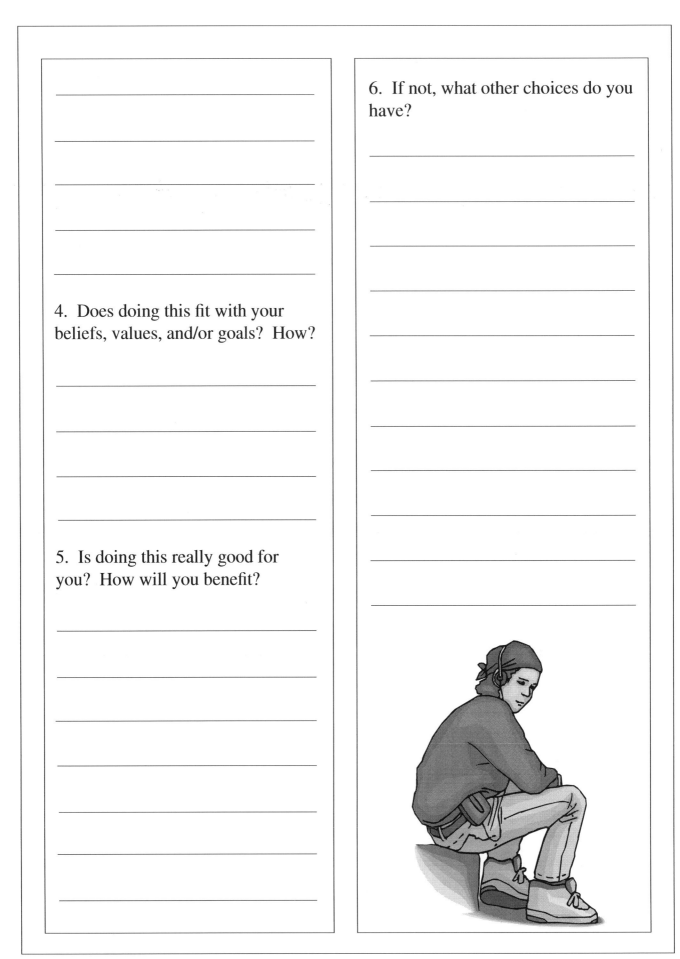

Responsibility & Community Involvement

A big part of being successful is learning how to be accountable — to take responsibility for the outcomes of your decisions. The first activity in this section gives you an opportunity to think about issues of responsibility and come to your own conclusions.

When should you begin to get involved in the community? Do you have to wait until you're finished with school? — or are there ways that you can contribute right now? In the book's final activity you'll have an opportunity to answer these questions.

You Be the Judge

Directions: Read the stories and answer the questions.

JUDY AND THE ORIOLES

The Orioles girls' softball team has been practicing after school at the park and winning most of its Saturday games. Judy is the best pitcher. The most important game of the season is coming up next weekend, a three-day holiday. It will determine which teams make the finals. Everything is going fine until Judy tells the girls on her team that for months her parents have been planning a camping trip for that weekend, and they expect her to go with them. The members of the team become angry and upset. They try to convince Judy to stay and pitch, but she says she's free to do as she pleases.

• Who is responsible for what? ...to whom?

_____

_____

• Is Judy responsible to the team, to her parents, or to herself?

_____

• Are Judy's parents responsible to the team?

_____

• Is it the coach's responsibility to persuade Judy's parents to cancel the trip or allow Judy to stay?

_____

• Was it Judy's responsibility to check the schedule and see that her parents were informed?

_____

• How much freedom should Judy have in this situation to decide what to do?

_____

_____

TONY'S FATHER QUITS

Tony's father has been a responsible worker on the same job for 15 years. Because of this, Tony has had a typical advantages of an upper-middle class student: clothes, money, and just about any other reasonable thing he needs or wants. Then one day, Tony's father suddenly announces that he hates what he's doing for a living. He says he can't take another day of it, quits his job, and takes a part-time position that pays far less money.

For years Tony has assumed that his father would buy him a new car for his 16th birthday, but that won't be possible now. In fact, his father tells him there will be no more allowances, and if he wants money for anything other than basic things like food, he will have to work for it himself. Tony protests. He insists that his father owes him an allowance and a car. He says his parents promised him these things. He also tells his father that he has no right to quit his job without checking with the rest of the family first. Tony's father says Tony is confused. He tells Tony that he is free to do what he wants.

• What basic responsibilities does Tony's father have to Tony and the rest of the family?

_____

_____

_____

• Does he really have the freedom or the right to quit his job?

_____

• Is he responsible to Tony to give him an allowance and buy him a car?

_____

_____

• What are his (the father's) responsibilities to himself?

_____

_____

_____

• Is Tony responsible as a family member to be kind and understanding during a difficult time in his father's life? Why or why not?

_____

_____

_____

_____

_____

KRONTZ FACES THE ADA

Samuel Krontz owns a small manufacturing and repair business that employs about 50 people. A few years ago, his business made large profits, but he and his board of directors invested the money unwisely and lost almost all of it. Now the business has a lot of competition; costs of production and salaries for workers are rising. The company is barely able to stay alive. Besides that, the physical plant is old, and there is not enough money to make needed improvements. The possibility of getting a large enough loan to do the job are very slim because of the company's poor credit rating.

As if to add insult to injury, the American Disabilities Act (ADA) has made it necessary for Mr. Krontz to widen entrance doors, add wheelchair ramps, remodel public restrooms, and face the likelihood of hiring workers with disabilities. And that's not all. In the past, if a worker suffered a serious illness or accident and couldn't return to his or her regular job before sick leave ran out, the worker would be terminated and a new person hired. Now Mr. Krontz will have to make "reasonable accommodations" to support workers who can't resume their normal workload after an illness like cancer. Rather than face these changes, Mr. Krontz and the board have started making plans to move his manufacturing business to Mexico, where he won't have to worry about laws like the ADA. He says it's the government's fault if 50 people are put out of work. He can do whatever he chooses.

• Should Mr. Krontz be free to do whatever he wants?

_____

• To whom is Mr. Krontz responsible, the 50 workers and their families, or himself and the company's board of directors?

_____

_____

• What would be the most responsible thing for him to do?

_____

_____

• Should he try to get a loan to make the physical changes required by the ADA, even though he won't get enough to remodel the plant completely?

_____

• Should he keep things as they are and take his chances?

_____

• What other solutions could he seek?

_____

_____

_____

A World of Opportunity

Some people think that there's a paying job for everything that needs to be done in our world. Not so. If it weren't for volunteer efforts, hundreds of problems would go unsolved, and thousands (perhaps millions) of people would have to do without the things they need to live decently —or to live at all. Help your class identify some of the problems that can be partially solved through volunteer community action. Complete these activities and share the information with your classmates.

Survey three adults. Ask each person these questions:

1. What is the biggest problem facing our nation today? What can each one of us, as an individual, do about it?
2. What are the two biggest problems facing our community today? What can each one of us, as an individual, do about them?

National Problem   **What We Can Do**

_____   _____

_____   _____

_____   _____

Community Problems   **What We Can Do**

1. _____   1. _____

_____   _____

_____   _____

2. _____   2. _____

_____   _____

_____   _____

Look through the newspaper. Find an article that describes a problem facing the world, the nation, or your community. It could be related to pollution, hunger, human rights, homelessness, crime, education, health care, efforts to find a cure for a specific disease, or some other issue. Read the article carefully to be sure you understand the problem.

Name three things that an organized group of citizens could do voluntarily that would help alleviate the problem.

1. _____

_____

_____

_____

2. _____

_____

_____

_____

_____

3. _____

_____

_____

_____

_____

In the space below, write the names of three community action organizations or volunteer agencies in your community. Briefly explain the purpose of each one.

Here are some suggestions for identifying the agencies: Use the telephone directory and ask people you know. Call the United Way, which represents many volunteer agencies. Don't guess the purpose of an agency. Contact the agency and ask the person who answers to explain the purpose to you, or use the internet to research the agency's purpose.

Organization 1: _____

Purpose: _____

_____

_____

Organization 2: _____

Purpose: _____

_____

_____

Organization 3: _____

Purpose: _____

_____

_____

_____

If your heart is in Social-Emotional
Learning, visit us online.

Come see us at
www.InnerchoicePublishing.com

Our web site gives you a look at all our other Social-Emotional
Learning-based books, free activities, articles, research, and
learning and teaching strategies. Every week you'll get a new
Sharing Circle topic and lesson.

INNERCHOICE Publishing

15079 Oak Chase Court
Wellington, FL 33414

Made in the USA
Lexington, KY
26 August 2014